THE COMPLETE GUIDE TO WRITING EFFECTIVE RÉSUMÉ COVER LETTERS:

Step-by-step Instructions with Companion CD-ROM

By Kimberly Sarmiento

The Complete Guide to Writing Effective Résumé Cover Letters: Step-by-step Instructions with Companion CD-ROM

Copyright © 2009 Atlantic Publishing Group, Inc.
1405 SW 6th Avenue • Ocala, Florida 34471 • Phone 800-814-1132 • Fax 352-622-1875
Web site: www.atlantic-pub.com • E-mail: sales@atlantic-pub.com
SAN Number: 268-1250

ISBN-13: 978-1-60138-238-2   ISBN-10: 1-60138-238-3

Library of Congress Cataloging-in-Publication Data

Sarmiento, Kimberly, 1975-
 The complete guide to writing effective résumé cover letters : step by step instructions, with companion CD-ROM / by Kimberly Sarmiento.
   p. cm.
Includes bibliographical references and index.
ISBN-13: 978-1-60138-238-2 (alk. paper)
ISBN-10: 1-60138-238-3 (alk. paper)
1. Cover letters. 2. Résumés (Employment) I. Title.
HF5383.S265 2009
650.14'2--dc22
                                    2009014392

PROJECT MANAGER: Amanda Miller • amiller@atlantic-pub.com
COVER DESIGN: Holly Marie Gibbs • hgibbs@atlantic-pub.com
INTERIOR DESIGN: Holly Marie Gibbs • hgibbs@atlantic-pub.com

We recently lost our beloved pet "Bear," who was not only our best and dearest friend but also the "Vice President of Sunshine" here at Atlantic Publishing. He did not receive a salary but worked tirelessly 24 hours a day to please his parents. Bear was a rescue dog that turned around and showered myself, my wife Sherri, his grandparents  Jean, Bob and Nancy and every person and animal he met (maybe not rabbits) with friendship and love. He made a lot of people smile every day.

We wanted you to know that a portion of the profits of this book will be donated to The Humane Society of the United States. *–Douglas & Sherri Brown*

The human-animal bond is as old as human history. We cherish our animal companions for their unconditional affection and acceptance. We feel a thrill when we glimpse wild creatures in their natural habitat or in our own backyard.

Unfortunately, the human-animal bond has at times been weakened. Humans have exploited some animal species to the point of extinction.

The Humane Society of the United States makes a difference in the lives of animals here at home and worldwide. The HSUS is dedicated to creating a world where our relationship with animals is guided by compassion. We seek a truly humane society in which animals are respected for their intrinsic value, and where the human-animal bond is strong.

Want to help animals? We have plenty of suggestions. Adopt a pet from a local shelter, join The Humane Society and be a part of our work to help companion animals and wildlife. You will be funding our educational, legislative, investigative and outreach projects in the U.S. and across the globe.

Or perhaps you'd like to make a memorial donation in honor of a pet, friend or relative? You can through our Kindred Spirits program. And if you'd like to contribute in a more structured way, our Planned Giving Office has suggestions about estate planning, annuities, and even gifts of stock that avoid capital gains taxes.

Maybe you have land that you would like to preserve as a lasting habitat for wildlife. Our Wildlife Land Trust can help you. Perhaps the land you want to share is a backyard— that's enough. Our Urban Wildlife Sanctuary Program will show you how to create a habitat for your wild neighbors.

So you see, it's easy to help animals. And The HSUS is here to help.

2100 L Street NW • Washington, DC 20037 • 202-452-1100 • www.hsus.org

DEDICATION

For Trish...I miss you.

To Ayla and Julian: I love you both!

TABLE OF CONTENTS

Chapter 10: Samples by Industry 177

FOREWORD

The Complete Guide to Writing Effective Résumé Cover Letters provides the reader with a step-by-step analysis of cover letter writing and exemplary examples to inspire readers of every profession. Kimberly Sarmiento has written a detailed, yet easy to follow guide that covers nearly every facet in cover letter creation.

With the state of the economy in flux and job opportunities becoming scarce, a powerful and effective cover letter is key in a successful career search. Human resource departments receive hundreds, perhaps thousands, of inquiries regarding their job postings. It is imperative that the cover letter captures the attention of the reader and quickly conveys qualification information.

This book uncovers the tools needed to craft an effective cover letter. It covers everything from the salutation of the cover letter to the keywords used in various industries. In this book, Kimberly Sarmiento's instructions will guide you in crafting your cover letter so that it will catch the attention of potential employers, and hopefully move you to the next phase of the job search — the interview.

Whether you find writing a difficult chore best avoided or a passion to indulge in, this book offers valuable advice that will make the task of cover letter writing seem easy. No matter where you are in your job search, *The Complete Guide to Writing Effective Résumé Cover Letters* will be an effective tool for you to use while creating a successful cover letter.

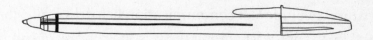

Introduction

How many hands have you shaken in the last week? How about in the last month? Just a few years ago, handshakes, meetings, and face-to-face conversations were the norm when it came to interacting with your fellow human beings. These days, you can converse, collaborate, and even complete a project with another individual without ever meeting them in person. The world has changed a great deal in the last decade. In the early '90s, the "Internet" was just a buzzword that computer science majors muttered while gathered around a circuit board. To most of us, the "Net" was something you used to chase a wayward guppy in an aquarium. By the end of that decade, Internet service providers began offering access for a monthly fee, rather than a price-per-minute bill, and public use exploded.

As the World Wide Web flooded into our homes, and other means of communication have become more prevalent, our lives have been quickly transformed, most notably in how we interact with each other. Handwritten correspondence was dubbed "snail mail" as e-mail, electronic bulletin boards, and blogs took over as our means of articulating our ideas. Web sites, graphical playgrounds for content, bombard your eyes and ears with information. You are more likely to get a text message nowadays telling you what time the meeting will be rather than a phone call.

The natural evolution of communication has drastically changed many things – not least among them is the process of submitting résumés and the role cover letters play in that process. Ten or fifteen years ago, the way your résumé physically looked, and even felt, was considered to be crucial. The weight and color of your paper and the font of your résumé was considered vitally important. Anything that would make the hiring director pause, as they rifled through the stacks of résumés, was a good thing. Nowadays, most résumés are submitted via e-mail or fax, negating those old methods of catching a hiring director's eye. So what can you do to make your résumé stand out in a sea of e-mails and faxes? The answer is simple: Write an outstanding cover letter.

When going to apply for a job you might think that a well-constructed résumé is the key to getting an interview. You might believe that the proper highlighting of your strengths, accomplishments, and special recognitions will be the most important thing to distinguish you from your competitors. Also, you probably spent a great deal of time assembling your résumé before you sat down and started looking for job openings. Then you read the line, "Interested applicants should send résumé and cover letter to jobs@jobopenings.com." If you wrote a quick, sloppy cover letter or sent your résumé off without one, you may have seriously handicapped your job search right from the start. All the hard work you have put into crafting that résumé may be wasted.

According to the Professional Résumé Writers Association, one-third of hiring directors will disqualify an applicant without a cover letter, one-third prefer to see a cover letter accompany a résumé, and only one-third will consider a résumé without one. That means 67 percent of potential employers expect to see a well-written cover letter along with your résumé. For the remaining 33 percent, it certainly can't hurt to send one as long as it is done well.

You might be scratching your head right now, wondering why cover letters have become so important. Well, the first thing to remember is that our current economy favors employers. Much like the housing market in 2009 is a "buyer's market," the job market today is a "hirer's market." HR departments may get hundreds, even thousands, of respondents to a job posting. Will they want to look at each one in detail? No.

"As the first step – we filter out," said Danny Huffman of Career Services International. Huffman is a professional résumé writer who specializes in portfolio management and career advancement. "Just because you can do the job doesn't mean you are the person they are going to pick to do the job," Huffman explained. Being qualified, even exceptionally qualified, is not the only thing companies are looking for today. That is why your résumé is not enough. "A cover letter affords the hiring executive the chance to get a feel that you are the right fit," said Huffman.

That leads to the second reason why cover letters have become so prominent in the job application process. Cover letters can often convey personality. Companies and their managers have come to realize that having a person who can do the job may not be enough. Personality, the ability to work and coexist with fellow employees, has become just as important as job skill. Corporate culture, as it has come to be known, can often make or break a company. If the employees can work together like a well-oiled machine, the company is often the better for it. Conversely, if there is dissidence and disharmony among the rank and file, that will lead to inefficiency, loss of revenue, and, in extreme cases, company downfall.

That is why the absence of a cover letter is a filter for so many hiring directors. A poorly written letter, with typos and other errors, will certainly filter you out as well. There is a widely regarded rule that we all hear dozens of times throughout our lives: You never get a second chance to make a good first impression. Your cover letter is your first impression to your prospective employer. Failing to make a positive impression could be the difference between getting an interview and your résumé being relegated to the recycle bin.

Perhaps the most daunting challenge a cover letter presents is that there is no generic, all-inclusive cover letter. Yes, a cover letter needs an introduction, a body, and a conclusion, but what goes in them? When conducting a job search, a person usually prepares one résumé that fits the needs of every position for which they apply. If the person is conducting a wide search, they might prepare a few résumés for different types of positions. But, the idea is still the same. The résumé is a generic document assembled and sent to multiple potential employers. This is not the case for a cover letter.

The cover letter is a tailored document targeted to a specific employment opportunity. Once you have selected your font and style, you might create a template for each cover letter that will allow you to save your contact information and signature. But there is no template for the content in a cover letter. You would not greet each potential employer with a plastic smile and a generic comment about their company and the job opening. Instead, you would tailor your comments to the person you were meeting and the position to which you were applying. You must do the same with each cover letter you prepare.

For some people, the task of finding a new job may seem exciting. For others, it might be a stressful, daunting process. No matter which describes you, it is unlikely the prospect of writing dozens – perhaps hundreds – of customized cover letters thrills you as you prepare to bombard the job market with your résumé. That is understandable. However, the process of writing cover letters can be fun. Where your résumé will be formal, your cover letter will be peppered with your personality. Once you have mastered the art of writing cover letters, the task of writing a personalized introduction to each potential employer will seem less like a chore and more like an outlet for self-expression.

With the understanding of how important cover letters are for your job search, the goal of this book is to help you accomplish two things:

1. Assemble the basics you need to write any cover letter for any position.

2. Turn that basic cover letter into a memorable introduction to your future employer.

To accomplish these goals, this book is laid out in three parts:

Part One: The Letter

There is a great deal that goes into writing a cover letter that makes an impact, but it is not a difficult process. The first thing this book will do is break down the cover letter into manageable parts that will remove intimidation and trepidation from the process. The first five chapters are dedicated to breaking down each part of the cover letter, from the introduction to the closing, and explaining how to effectively craft each section to form a cohesive whole.

Part Two: Packaging

The second part of this book will focus on how to take that simple cover letter that introduces you to your potential employer and make it the most memorable introduction possible. When you walk in for your interview, you will want your hair perfect, your suit lint-free, and your shoes polished and shining. That is the visual image we want your employer to summon when they read your stand-out cover letter. The section includes several chapters focused on formatting, design, wording, phrasing, and other details that will make your cover letter as dynamic and engaging as possible.

Part Three: Samples

Throughout the book, sample cover letters are used to illustrate specific points. In part three, you will see dozens of "total package" cover letters to give you a greater feel for how all the advice and components of this book fit together. Additionally, there are several chapters dedicated to offering specific recommendations based on experience, industry, and special circumstances.

PART ONE

THE LETTER

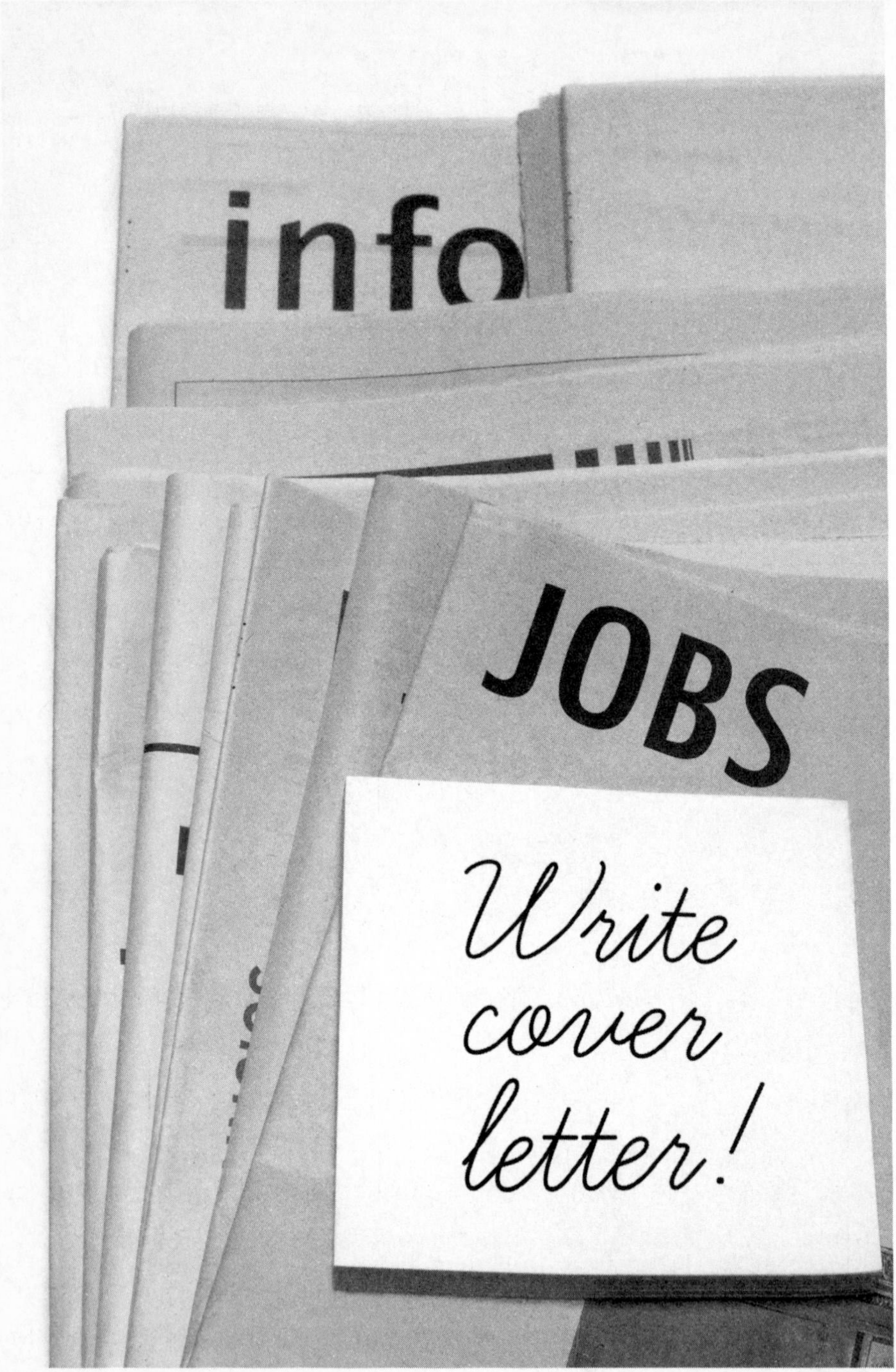
info
JOBS
Write cover letter!

CHAPTER 1

Cover Letter Basics

One of the pluses of the cover letter is that it is a creative, personal document, and when you are being creative – generally speaking – anything goes. However, within the realm of creativity there are guidelines that most people follow. A painter does not usually use a rock to apply paint to paper. A musician has to follow the basics of rhythm and time when composing a song. Along that same idea, there are three basic "rules" for writing cover letters.

Three Basic Rules for Cover Letters:

Rule 1: Cover letters should be to the point and make an impact.

There was a time when the general consensus for most résumés was that they should be limited to one sheet of paper. Since HR departments often had to sort, stack, and look over hundreds, if not thousands of résumés, multi-paged résumés were impractical at best. Nowadays, résumés are often transmitted and stored electronically, and that old maxim has been discarded in favor of résumés with more detailed descriptions of job histories and skill sets.

Cover letters, on the other hand, should still be limited to **a single page**.

First off, the human resource personnel or hiring authority reading your cover letter will be using it to make a quick assessment. You have seconds, not minutes, to make an impression. If your reader has to flip a page or scroll down very far on their computer screen, chances are good that they will stop reading. Your cover letter should be cliff notes, not the novel.

Think about this: When you first meet someone, do you instantly hammer them with information about yourself? Well, some people might. But, generally speaking, you will exchange some pleasantries, get a feel for each other, and then dive into more detail about yourselves. Think of your cover letter as those "pleasantries," while your résumé contains your details. Your résumé and cover letter should work together to get you past that initial screening process and into an interview.

Another reason cover letters should be limited to one page is that honestly they are a test of your abilities. Can you capture your reader's attention? How quickly can you do it? Can you briefly describe yourself, your skills, and show why you are right for the job, while being constrained to such a limited space? Your ability to do this may demonstrate your ability to sell to a customer, present information at a meeting, or give instructions to a team. The hiring authority is accessing more than what goes into your cover letter; they are accessing how well you wrote it. That is why it is important to do more than write a short cover letter. You must write one that makes an impact, as well.

Rule 2: Your cover letter and résumé should complement each other.

While your cover letter will be tailored for the specific position you are applying to, it must be a reflection of your résumé each and every time you submit one. It should include several highlights from your résumé that you want to bring to the forefront. It should also look like your résumé.

To ensure that your résumé and cover letter are unitary documents, you will want them to have visual similarities. Use the same font type, size, and header. When printing the documents, put them on matching high-quality paper. These details may seem small and inconsequential on the surface, but anything you can do to make your cover letter and résumé stand out positively is a good thing.

Conversely, your cover letter should generally not contain information that is not contained in your résumé. There are exceptions to this rule. There may come a time when a hobby (like photography or Web page design) can demonstrate skills needed for a position for which you have no workplace experience. In those instances, bringing up something that is not captured on your résumé can serve a vital function in your cover letter. However, most of the time, you will want to take a few highlights from your résumé and delve deeper into them as you write your cover letter.

Rule 3: Show attention to detail.

One day I was teasing a guy friend about his abundant amount of shoes. He did not simply tell me that I had an unusually low amount for a woman or that some of his shoes were over ten years old (which was the response I was expecting). No, what I got was actually an incredibly lengthy explanation about the importance of men's shoes when that man is on the dating market. Surprised? So was I. In response, I commented that you would likely eliminate quality life mates if you judged a person by the quality of their shoes. He agreed, but not before he made me admit that we all judge people to some degree on their appearance. It might not be fair, but people use visual cues to sum up what type of date you would be.

Hiring authorities do the same thing for employees. From our shoes (some managers don't want to see women in open-toed shoes, while others expect men to be in dress shoes, not loafers), to our clothing (suits and ties are expected at some establishments, while others are more casual), to our physical appearance (e.g., hair, tattoos, piercings, jewelry, and make-up), interviewers are making quick decisions about you based on the way you look, as well as what you say, in an interview.

But your first visual cue to a hiring authority doesn't take place at your initial interview. It takes place in your cover letter. Part two of this book delves into how you can make that visual cue as appealing as possible. However, the basic cue you must send your employer is that you pay attention to details.

For example, when you are e-mailing a cover letter, your e-mail will be time-stamped by the receiver's e-mail system. You do not want to have the date on your cover letter heading to be too far from that stamp. The point is, you do not want to make it seem like you are recycling letters (you may very well be, but do not let them know that!). Do not send a cover letter that was dated a month ago. You want to give the perception that your cover letter was recently written because the job you are applying for is at the top of your priority list. Small details can make big impressions.

Use a spelling and grammar checker. Read it. Re-read it. Read it again. Have someone else read your cover letter, if need be, but do not submit a cover letter with spelling or grammatical errors. No one is going to take your application seriously if you have not taken the time to make sure your one page cover letter is free of mistakes. This really cannot be emphasized enough. "Ain't" might have a place in the dictionary now, but it should not be present in your cover letter.

Do research. Identify the person who might be reading your cover letter. Address your letter to them. Find out the address of the company; include this in your header. Make sure you have an appropriate salutation. Ensure that you meet all the requirements the job posting has requested. All these things will be touched on in greater detail in the subsequent chapters. Just remember that details are crucial in writing a good cover letter.

If possible, find out some information about the company and the industry they are in. You will not want to spend a great deal of your precious one-page document revealing what you know of the company, but you want to at least convey that you have looked them up and are aware of what they do. A blurb or two will often suffice, and will give the hiring authority the impression that you have an idea of what the company is about and want to be a part of it.

Types of Cover Letters

Once you understand the basic guidelines to follow when writing cover letters, you must then decide what type of cover letter you are writing. Who is your audience? What do you intend for this cover letter to convey? Ultimately, in every cover letter you are asking for an interview. But the details of that request, and the method by which it is delivered, may vary significantly.

One book might tell you there are four types of cover letters. Another might tell you there are ten. It can be a little confusing and altogether intimidating as you are trying to get started. This book will examine four basic types of cover letters. In an extensive job search, it is very likely you will prepare a cover letter from each category. So, it important to recognize the differences in each, since the tone and substance of your cover letter may vary greatly depending on your audience.

Below is a brief description of each type of cover letter. Chapter two will delve into specific recommendations for writing each of those letters and address the components that are unique to each of them.

The Solicited Response:

The first category of cover letters is the one that probably springs to mind immediately when you think of sending out your résumé – those sent out as a response to an advertised position.

In this type of letter, you will specifically highlight how your talents meet the requirements advertised in the job listing. You can think of this as the "best fit" cover letter. A company is looking for a certain individual with a certain skill set, and you will demonstrate to them that you are their "best fit."

Letters to a Headhunter:

The second type of cover letter you will likely produce is one to a headhunter or recruitment agency. The purpose of this cover letter is to give the headhunter a fairly good summary of your skill set and what you are looking for in terms of employment so they, in turn, can sell you to one of their clients.

With any luck, the cover letter you prepare for a headhunter will be one that is following up on a contact they made to you. But, if that is not the case, you may still submit a cover letter to a recruiting agency, unsolicited or in response to an advertisement.

These letters are slightly more generic than the ones prepared in response to an advertised position, but there may be information you would include in these that would not go into the first type of cover letter. For example, you may include specific salary requirements or locations you prefer to work. The purpose of this type of cover letter is to give the headhunter an accurate accounting of your skills and abilities so they can present you in the best light to their audience, your prospective employers.

"Cold-Call" Letters:

The third type of cover letter you may produce is that which will accompany an unsolicited résumé. Often referred to as "cold call" letters, these may include networking letters, referral letters, or broadcast cover letters.

A networking letter is one where you are contacting professional and personal contacts, asking whether they know of any job openings in your area of expertise.

A referral letter is one where you address your letter and résumé to someone who has been suggested to you by a friend or colleague.

The broadcast cover letter is one where you seek to advertise to a company that you are on the job market, in hopes they will have a position that you would be qualified to fill.

Online Cover Letters:

The fourth type of cover letter that you might compose is the one that will be attached to an online résumé. **Monster.com**, Yahoo Hotjobs, and many other Web sites will allow you to upload and submit a résumé online for employers to review. They will ask if you would like to submit a cover letter along with that résumé. You do not have to include a cover letter with your online profile, but it is often a good idea, as it is a good way of conveying your personality to potential employers or recruiters who review those sites looking for résumés that fill their requirements.

These are probably the most generic cover letters you will write. Since you are not targeting a specific job posting or company, you will emphasize your skill sets in the hopes they catch an HR person's eye. These types of letters can often be the easiest, and, at the same time, the most challenging to write. While on one hand, it would be easy enough to write down what you can do and where you came from, you need to take care that your cover letter does not become a simple laundry list of your skill sets and experience. Remember, the purpose of a cover letter is to inform and engage. These letters are difficult to write because you do not know who will be reading them. So you will need to be fairly broad in your scope, but still captivating enough to capture the interest of a hiring director while they are skimming through an online database.

Cover Letter Components

No matter which of the above cover letters you are composing, they will all have these seven basic elements in common:

- Contact information

- Date

- Address/Salutation

- Opening paragraph

- Content

- Closing paragraph

- Signature

Subsequent chapters will go into a detailed analysis for the opening, content, and closing paragraphs. The remainder of this chapter will delve into the four remaining elements of your cover letter.

Contact Information:

Contact information might seem like an obvious thing to include in your cover letter, but you would be surprised how often this information gets omitted. When that happens, the excellent cover letter and résumé you have prepared gets sent to the recycle bin or trash can, where it can do you no good. Do not assume that just because your return address is on an envelope, or that they can reply to your e-mail, that a human resource director or hiring manager will make the effort to do those things. In fact, it is unlikely they will even read your cover letter or résumé if you leave off this most basic information.

Additionally, please do not think that just because this information is on your résumé, you do not need to include it on your cover letter. Your cover letter is what the HR person or hiring manager will see first. Do not ever give them a reason to discard your application. Treat your cover letter as if it is as important as your résumé, because it is.

Besides, it is easy to include your contact information, because this is one of the few elements of your cover letter that you can save in a template and use time and time again. In fact, it is best to use the exact same heading as the one used on your résumé. If, for some reason, you wish not to do that, make sure your cover letter matches your résumé in font style and size. Keep the contact information in the same order for each document (if you list your phone number above your e-mail address on your résumé, keep it the same on your cover letter). Once again, this relates to attention to detail. But also, the person reading your cover letter will know how easy it is for you to include this information. The absence of it could make you appear lazy, unorganized, not detail oriented, or unfamiliar with what is expected of you professionally. Do not leave a bad impression by letting this valuable component of your cover letter get left out.

Contact information should include the following:

Name
Mailing address
Phone number(s)
E-mail address

Name:

You are probably laughing a little to yourself right now thinking, "Come on. I might need a book to tell me how to write a cover letter, but I do know my name!"

That is true. You do know your name. But your future employer does not, and many times, people go by a name other than their proper legal name.

If you use your middle name instead of your first, or if you are a "Bob" instead of a Robert, or a "Beth" instead of an Elizabeth, consider the following suggestions:

Angela S. "Susan" Miller
Gunther H. "Henry" Jones
Patricia "Trish" Wallace
Jonathan "Jack" Webb

The last thing you want a hiring director to do is pick up the phone to reach Harriet Mills and hear, "Hi there. This is Sue. Sorry I missed you. Leave your message at the beep and I will get back to you." It is very likely that Harriet Susan Mills will never receive the message asking her to call back to schedule an interview for that job.

Mailing address:

Generally speaking, just include your complete mailing address, with apartment number if applicable. Post office boxes are acceptable, and sometimes very useful, especially if you are in transition. That is because one of the times in life when we need to job hunt the most is also one of the times when our address is in flux – when we are relocating.

If you already know your future address, or if you have a permanent address you are using for contact information (like a student away at school or a spouse following behind someone who has already relocated), try using the following example:

JOHN H. SMITH

JohnS3357@email.com

Permanent Address:	Current Address:
5555 Strong Road	Emerson Hall Rm. 555
Orlando FL 34877	University of Florida
Cell: (407) 555-5555	Gainesville FL 37849

If, on the other hand, you know you are going to be moving, but do not know your future contact information yet, it is best that you inform your potential employers of your relocation and give them a phone number and e-mail that will be available to you in your transition.

Do not include a phone number that will be discontinued after your move.

Do not include an e-mail address that you will no longer have access to because you are switching providers.

Both of these problems are easily addressed. Even if you do not make it a practice to carry a cell phone, you can obtain an inexpensive, no-obligation, pay-as-you-go cell phone to list as your contact number. You can take this phone with you as you transition, and when you no longer have need of it, you can let the minutes on it expire and discard it.

For your e-mail address, you should register with one of the many providers that give out free e-mail addresses, such as Yahoo, Windows Live, or Google. Then you can access that e-mail address wherever you go, even if you must use a local library until your Internet connection is established at your new residence.

Phone number:

Do not give out your work phone number. Even if your employer knows you are job hunting and you think it will not hurt anything, do not do it. It is best to give out a cell phone, or home phone number, but even as you do that, be careful that whatever voice message your potential employer receives if they do not reach you is professional and accurately identifies you.

As mentioned in the "name" section, you want to make sure your cover letter accurately identifies what name you go by. Once you have done that, you need to make sure any message an interview scheduler receives is professional and verifies that they have reached the correct person. Your friends may think it is cute or funny if you sound like you inhaled a balloon full of helium on your greeting, but it does not seem particularly professional. Ignore this last statement if you are applying to be a clown in the circus.

Additionally, you do not want them to hear your 3-year-old singing "Twinkle, Twinkle Little Star" before your voice comes over the recording to say, "Leave us a message. Beep." You also do not want them to call your cell phone to hear "Hey there. You know who it is. If you don't – hang up. If you do – tell me what you want."

People get nervous when recording messages or they see them as an opportunity to be funny and unique. There is a time for that, but not when you are receiving messages from future employers. Instead, try: "Hi there. This is Trish Wallace. I'm sorry I missed your call. Please leave me a message with your name and reason for calling, and I will get back with you as soon as possible. Thank you, and have a wonderful day."

Yes, it is dry and a bit dull, but it is also professional and conveys the information you want a potential employer to hear. When you land the job, go buy a dozen balloons and have some fun.

When listing your phone number in your contact information, it is unnecessary to type the word "phone."

Example:

> John Smith
> 2836 West Main St.
> Any town, MI 5847
> Phone: (675) 555-4832

Doing so is unnecessary and can sometimes make a bad impression, according to Danny Huffman of Career Services International. Your reader knows that it is a phone number, explained

Huffman. Tacit information — information which is implied or already known — should be edited from your cover letter, he said. This starts with your contact information. Instead, simply list your phone number or specify what type of phone you are listing.

Example:

Jane Smith
3896 Orange Tree Blvd.
Littletown, AL 48373
(456) 555-3948

Or:

Jane Smith
3896 Orange Tree Blvd.
Littletown, AL 48373
Cell: (456) 555-3948
Home: (456) 555-9387

E-mail:

E-mail is not just important for people looking to relocate; it is important for anyone on the job-hunting scene. This form of communication has exploded to the point that some people without phones will have e-mail addresses. Chances are very good you will submit most of your cover letters/résumés by e-mail. It might serve you well to get a free e-mail account from MSN, Yahoo, or Google that is completely dedicated to your job search. This will help you archive which companies you have already contacted, which recruiters you have already been in touch with, and which ads you have already responded to. These e-mail providers also have the advantage of being web based; that is, as long as you can get access to the Internet, you can get to your e-mail from anywhere in the world. This is especially important if you are relocating. It might take a few days or so to travel to your new location, or it might take a few days to get your access set up at your new home. A quick trip to a local library or Internet café will let you check to see if any prospective employers are looking to get a hold of you.

Much like your phone message, your e-mail address should be professional as well. Do not use sexygirl65@email.com or bad-boyonwheels78@email.com. It is perfectly understandable that your e-mail address might not have your full name included in it, but it should not stand out for reasons of being lewd or immature.

Much like your phone listing should not include the word "phone," Huffman says you should not include the word "e-mail" in your contact information either. Additionally, he suggests making sure the hyperlink in your e-mail address is turned off when you submit your cover letter and résumé. This is a "turn off" to a small percentage of hiring executives, he explained. And while it might not be significant to your reader, it is better to play it safe. Plus, being able to turn it off demonstrates a small amount of computer know-how.

If you are using a Word-compatible program, the program may automatically format e-mail addresses that you type as hyperlinks. If you want to turn off this option, you can do so in Microsoft Word 2003 by going to the "Tools" menu and selecting

"AutoCorrect Options" then the "AutoFormat as You Type" tab. Under "Replace as You Type," clear the "Internet and network paths with hyperlinks" checkbox to disable that option. In Windows Vista, you can simply right-click on the e-mail address and select the option "Remove hyperlink." If you have a Mac or any other word processing software, please make sure you know how to turn this feature off.

If you are pasting or typing your cover letter directly into an e-mail, some programs may allow you to right-click on the link and disable it. However, some Web-based e-mail programs may not have this option. So, the best way is to use the plain text formatting option, which will remove hyperlinks. This may, however, remove some formatting you have done in Word. Therefore, you will have to carefully review a pasted cover letter when doing this.

Once you have assembled all the data that you want to put into your contact information, you just need to decide on the format and then you can save it as a template to use over and over again.

Here are some examples:

Elizabeth Smith
3333 Martin Hwy.
Thomas Town, FL 56575
Home (354) 555-6498 / Cell (354) 555-8389 / esmith@email.com

JENNIFER JONES

4422 Smith Street   (456) 555-6490
Nunsville, PA 49830   jjones@email.com

Gordan R. "Robert" Jones
7849 North Center Street
West Bend, WI 58939

grjones@email.com
Residence: (489) 555-9899
Mobile: (478) 555-9878

SAMATHA ROBERTSON

1000 SW Orange Street – Sacramento, California 97844
966-555-7653 – slrobertson73@email.com

Mark Washington, Operations Manager
888 South Lincoln Ave. Atlanta, GA 47379 (706) 555-8373
markwashington68@email.com

Margaret "Peg" Mitchell

393 West 5th Street – Bloomburg, CT 23728 – (284) 555-2929

Date:

This is probably the second-easiest component of your cover letter. What could be easier than dating a letter? Make sure you are not dating it with the wrong year, and you are good to go, right? Well, almost.

As mentioned under the "attention to detail" section, you want the date of your letter to be close to the date that will be time-stamped on your e-mail/fax or the postmark that will be stamped on your envelope. You do not want it to appear that you are recycling cover letters and just changing the names. Nor do you want it to appear that your job search lacks urgency because you let your cover letter/résumé lay around on your desk for days or weeks before you sent it out.

This is a very small thing, but when you are competing against dozens if not hundreds of applicants for a position, every little thing counts.

Address/Salutation:

The inside address of your cover letter will usually include the complete name, title, and business address of the individual to whom you are addressing your letter.

Example:

Mr. Ben Nobles
General Sales Manager
Dollar General
1254 North Atlanta Blvd.
Jacksonville FL 34875

However, often you will not know that much information. You are far more likely to be responding to an e-mail address or fax number. If that is the case, modify the above example to one of the two examples below:

Mr. Ben Nobles   Mr. Ben Nobles
General Sales Manager   General Sales Manager
bnobles@email.com   Fax (950) 555-5847

Your salutation is simply the opening greeting you extend in your cover letter - The "Dear Mr. Smith" or "Dear Ms. Jones" of your letter. (Note that you should refer to all women as "Ms." unless you have specifically heard someone refer to them as "Mrs.")

Many experts will tell you to never use a "To Whom it May Concern" type of address to open your cover letter. There will be times when you will have no choice. The circumstances will depend greatly on what type of cover letter you are writing, and what information is available to you.

When introducing yourself for a job opening where the advertisement deliberately excludes identifying information, you will have no choice but to use generic greetings like "Dear Sir/Ma'am" or "Dear Hiring Authority," but you should try to minimize those times as much as possible.

Between your address and the salutation, some people will choose to insert a reference line. This is done specifically for cover letters that are responding to an advertised job listing. You can include this information in your opening paragraph. However, if you choose to insert a reference line, it will usually read something like this:

Mr. Ben Nobles

General Sales Manager

Dollar General

1254 North Atlanta Blvd.

Jacksonville FL 34875

Re: Second shift manager at S. Street location (posting 98342).

Dear Mr. Nobles:

Signature:

Your signature is the easiest thing to include in your cover letter. All you need to do is be consistent. Use the same name in your signature that you do in your contact information.

You may want to note beneath your name if you have included enclosures, but if you have mentioned that in your cover letter body, it is not necessary.

CHAPTER 2

Four Types of Cover Letters

Chapter one showed you how to get started cover letter writing. We touched on the basics of what should be in every cover letter. You can take the skills you learned in that chapter – the assembly of contact information, for example – and apply them to every cover letter you write.

The elements discussed in chapter one are vitally important to constructing a cover letter that makes an impact and leaves the reader impressed with not only the content of the letter, but the attention to detail shown in it. However, excelling at those elements will not win you that coveted interview. Indeed, perfecting those elements of the cover letter will merely keep you from an early elimination in the consideration process.

What secures your next step in the review process is how well you can add to the basic structure you have learned about in chapter one. How do you add "spice" to the dish, so to speak? The opening, the content, and the closing paragraph are the parts of the cover letter that will make the greatest impression on your reader. To write those paragraphs exceptionally well, you must first know your audience. By knowing your audience, you know what type of cover letter you will be writing.

This chapter will examine four types of cover letters that are targeting to very different audiences. The goal of each letter is to progress the candidate in the job consideration process, but the substance and tone of each letter may vary greatly, depending on your audience. Who you are talking to will make a significant difference in the information that needs to be included in each letter. In the sections below, we will delve into what each audience may need to hear from you.

The Solicited Response

This is a cover letter that accompanies a résumé being sent in response to an advertisement for a specific job opening. For this type of cover letter, you must keep in mind that:

Your skills should match their listed requirements.

Since these are the only cover letters where you will have detailed information provided by the company of the job requirements for which you are applying, it is vitally important that you tailor your cover letter so that it highlights specifically how your skills meet their needs.

Some advertisements that you come across on the Internet and in newspapers will list extremely specific job requirements. Consider the following example:

Company Name:	*HireAdvantage, Inc.*
Job Category:	*Technology; Banking/Mortgage*
Location:	*Smithsmoore, CA*
Position Type:	*Contract-to-Hire*
Experience:	*5-7 Years*
Date Posted:	*Jan. 30, 2009*

Description:

We are seeking a software engineer with a strong programming and systems integration background using Java, C/C++. We need the software engineer to design our core payment processing system. Design work includes engineering specifications and Internet design documents. Candidates must have extensive experience in the software development life cycle. Applicants should possess a degree in computer science with experience with other payment processing software.

Other requirements include:

- *Minimum of five years experience in a Java programming background.*
- *Application architecture and development experience in a transaction-processing environment.*
- *Applicants must demonstrate excellent written and oral communication skills and must be capable of interacting frequently with customers when needed.*
- *Applicant must be a self-starter who can interact in a collaborative environment with colleagues across departments.*
- *Applicant must be familiar with payment processing and ACH protocols.*

If you meet these qualifications and are interested in applying, please forward your résumé and cover letter to terri@email.com for review.

The following cover letter **body** illustrates how to translate the specific job requirements listed in the advertisement to your skills and experience:

With 14 years of experience in various coding methodologies and languages, I will design your core payment processing system in a way that is both user-friendly and dependable. I worked as an assistant manager for five years at Radio Shack as I earned a dual degree in computer engineering and business administration. In that time, I consistently led my store in sales, proving my ability to relate effectively to customers.

My additional qualifications include:

- *My second job out of college was for a software company whose products monitored and audited large credit card transactions for major retailers. I gained a great deal of experience in ACH systems and protocols in this position.*

- *I am well versed with Java and other OO-related programming. One of my Java related projects involved developing a thin client that was essentially a web based wrapper around one of our product interfaces.*

- *My excellent writing skills were honed in my work as a technical writer, having produced several of the manuals that have accompanied a slew of our products.*

- *At my current job, I was lead developer on several projects, and architected the back-end SQL database for our data warehousing software.*

I meet deadlines early and pride myself as a colleague that my co-workers can both rely and lean on. I believe that a good leader sets an example and is an encouraging voice in the work environment. I look forward to meeting with you to discuss how my skills can immediately serve your needs.

Other advertisements might be less detailed in their job requirements. Consider the following example:

Company: The Smallville Press
Position: Full-time reporter
Location: Smallville MD
Job Status: Full-time
Salary: $30,000-$35,000
Ad expires: March 10, 2009
Job ID: 1098

Description:

The Smallville Press, a 20,000 circulation daily newspaper in Smallville, MD, has an immediate opening for an experienced journalist to cover city government, entertainment, and community events. We like to have fun, work hard, and we believe any stories affecting our communities are worth telling. As our reporter, you'll be expected to produce daily stories and work on occasional special sections. We're a rural county located 90 miles west of Baltimore. This isn't a big city, but we offer great weather, good people, and outdoor recreation. We want a self-starter who gets the facts right, produces clean copy, knows how to generate quality stories, can post to the web, and take photographs as needed. This is a Sunday through Thursday shift with some evening events and meetings. Requirements include newspaper reporting experience, a college degree or its equivalent, a sense of humor, and someone who enjoys getting out in the community and meeting people. Send five to ten of your best clips showing hard news and feature writing to: Richard Thomas, Editor, The Smallville Press 2984 Main Street Smallville MD 21839. E-mail rthomas@email. com No phone calls please.

The following cover letter body demonstrates how to highlight your strengths for such an advertisement:

It was with great interest that I read about your opening for a full-time reporter on JobWebsite.com. The position sounds just perfect for someone who enjoys multi-tasking like myself! It is with great enthusiasm that I am submitting my résumé and writing samples for your review.

My experience and skills make me an excellent candidate for this position. I have worked as both a beat reporter for local government, covering city and county commission meetings, and as a feature reporter for the living section of my hometown newspaper, with a circulation of 25,000 readers.

I enjoyed freelancing while I earned my B.S. in Journalism from the University of Florida, and thanks to an excellent photo journalism course, I have dabbled in photography and Photoshop editing ever since. I am an avid Web user and even have my own Web site, which you can visit at www.website.com.

I believe that I am well qualified for this position, and I believe you will agree after you read the writing sample I have included. I hope we have an opportunity to meet in person to further discuss the details of this job opening.

Provide the information the advertisement requests:

While it is not necessarily a part of the cover letter, if a job listing, like the one above, makes specific requests in the advertisement, you should do your best to meet them. The posting above asked for "five to ten of your best clips showing hard news and feature writing." Obviously, these would not be in your cover letter. However, you can allude to those postings with a sentence or two in your letter.

Based on that request, anyone applying to this position should provide at least five writing samples that showcase the content the advertisement requested. To send less would indicate you lack the depth of experience the newspaper wants. To send writing samples that do not cover the topics they requested shows you lack experience in that field. If those situations arise, an explanation of what you have enclosed and why should be provided in your cover letter.

Many advertisements, like the one above, will provide you with a salary range the employer is willing to pay for that position. Some will say that pay will be determined based on experience. Salary might always be a negotiable issue to address after your second or third interview, but it is not necessary to address in your cover letter unless the advertisement specifically asks for you to provide your salary requirements, like the listing below does:

Company: All American Publishing, Inc.
Position: Editor
Location: NYC, New York
Job Status: Full-Time

Salary: Not Specified
Ad expires: March 10, 2009
Job ID: 1855

*Entertainment Web site focusing on news is seeking experienced editors who know how to break news and find new details on stories that have already broken. Experience a must. The right candidate will know how to direct a team of reporters and photographers, will understand that speed and accuracy are mandatory, and will have excellent entertainment and news contacts. We are looking for a tireless self-starter to step in and take control at a high-level position. Positions are based in NYC. **Please send résumé and salary requirements to: myrésuménvc@ email.com.***

When this question arises, most people become wary and start to mildly panic in the search for a proper response, wanting to neither lowball their figure, thus decreasing their earning potential, nor submit a number significantly higher than they are willing to accept and risk eliminating themselves from competition. In this scenario, it is best to use a range when answering this question to minimize your chances of scaring your prospective employer with an egregious sum or ending up working for a fraction of what your work is actually worth.

Addressing the Hiring Authority:

As discussed briefly in chapter one's section on salutations, it is commonly advised that you address your letter to a person by name, like "Ms. Rene Jones," rather than a position, like "To the Hiring Authority." But there are times when you will not have a choice. You will face advertisements where it is impossible to find out who the hiring director is or even the company/person you are applying for a position with.

Consider the following example:

SYSTEM ADMINISTRATOR – *Democratic Senator is seeking a Systems Administrator for a fast-paced office. Responsibilities include updating and maintaining network hardware and software, developing and maintaining an information management system for the office, maintaining computer security, and providing computer assistance and training as needed. Individual must be well-organized, detail-oriented, and able to work independently. Experience with Web site maintenance and content management is a plus. A bachelor's degree in computer engineering is highly desired. Position is based in D.C. Please e-mail cover letter and résumé to senateemployment@email.com and include reference number in the subject line.*

In cases such as this, a generic salutation is acceptable, but make sure that you do not miss clues given in advertisements that do not specifically list whom you would be applying with.

Consider this example:

DEFENSE INTERN – *Senior Florida Senator seeks part-time, paid intern for three-to-six-month internship. Responsibility will include assisting a busy national security staff with general administrative duties. Intern will also be expected to assist the staff in preparing the Senator for hearings, meetings, and travel. Strong research skills will be required since intern will also aide in tracking legislation and budget requests. A qualified candidate will be a recent college graduate or grad student who demonstrates attention to detail and excellent oral and written communication skills.*

*This internship is designed to give the intern Capitol Hill experience and the opportunity to transition into full-time employment is available. **Please submit cover letter, résumé, and 3-5 page writing sample via e-mail at: FloridaDefenseIntern@email.com. No calls please.***

While the advertisement does not specify the Florida senator by name, it does tell you it is the Senior Florida Senator looking to hire for this position. For those unaware of political lingo, the Senior Senator in each state is the one who was elected earliest. It would not take a great deal of research to discover that the Senior Senator from Florida is currently Bill Nelson.

It may at times be unavoidable to use generic opening lines, but make sure you make every effort to personalize a cover letter as much as possible before you do so.

Letters to a Headhunter or Recruiter

This cover letter is one that will be addressed to a headhunter or recruitment agency. Unlike the previous cover letter, you should not have a time when this cover letter gets addressed with a generic salutation. While some recruitment agencies might have several people working one area, it is best to go ahead and research the company well enough that you can address someone by name. A quick phone call will often yield at least one contact person. If that person's work load is too heavy or you are looking for a position out of their area, they can refer you to one of their colleagues.

If you are preparing to skim over this section – don't. Headhunters are a valuable resource in your job hunting campaign. This is an entire industry that is catered to matching companies with prospective employees. Be sure to take advantage of it. Only networking (personal contact at a company) is more successful in finding you a job. Therefore, you should look through your phone book and online and find the names of at least a couple of headhunting firms that specialize in placing people with your experience and skills and send them your résumé.

In the cover letter that accompanies that résumé, you will need to provide information that will likely not be included in any other type of cover letter, including your job search objectives, compensation requirements (they need to know at least a ballpark salary range when matching you to companies), and geographical/relocation preferences or restrictions.

You will also want to highlight what makes you a valuable asset to the companies for which they recruit. Since you will not have a specific listing to go off of, you will simply have to decide which are your greatest skills and accomplishments and design your letter to show off those attributes.

Remember that headhunters/recruiters have one main job function: match a company's hiring criteria to the perfect job candidate. Be straightforward with them. It makes their job easier and makes them more motivated to work for you. Feeding incorrect or inaccurate information only makes their work harder, and can expose them to potential embarrassment. Do not tell them you know how to build a computer if all your work experience has been in carpentry. Ensure that your cover letter is informative, accurate, and gives a headhunter a good overall picture of your skills and personality.

Consider the example on the following page:

John Smith
3333 Martin Hwy.
Thomas Town, FL 56575
Home (354) 555-6498 / Cell (354) 555-8389 / jsmith@email.com

January 1, 2009

Mr. Ben Anderson
Tech Placement Agency
1254 North Atlanta Blvd.
Jacksonville FL 34875

Dear Mr. Anderson:

Thank you for taking the time to look over this letter. I came across your headhunting agency in my efforts to find a new position. It appears that your company emphasizes placing people in technology firms, and that is exactly my background. I would love the opportunity to come in and meet with you to see if you have any clients that would be interested in my skills.

I have been in the technology industry for over 15 years. I have a bachelor's degree in Computer Information Systems, and have recently held a product manager position at ABC software. I have a strong background in Web application development, with experiences in both Java and Visual Basic. Due to my CIS degree, my former employers chose to utilize my project management training to help initialize, guide, and complete several software development projects. My last project involved designing a subway kiosk system that passengers could enter information regarding the best routes to their destination. I led a team of four programmers, one software architect, and two quality assurance engineers. Through our efforts, we were able to secure a 2.8 million dollar contract with the New York transit authority to implement and maintain this subway system near the Manhattan section of the New York subway. In addition to my product management background, I also have experience in photography and graphics design. I currently hold several Photoshop certifications, as well as being a contract photographer for one of my local newspapers. I have contributed some photo art to several recording artists' Web sites, most notably Dave Matthews Band's current Web site logo. I love the ability to merge my creative passions with the digital medium, and I feel I can offer a unique set of skills to many of your clients.

In conclusion, I hope I have given you a small glimpse of my abilities. I have attached my résumé, which gives a more detailed view of what my experiences are, and the skills I bring to the table. I feel that my mix of ability, creativity, and personality enhances any work environment that I am a part of and look forward to my next career opportunity. Please be advised that my target salary range is $60,000-$70,000. I am willing to travel, but cannot consider relocation at this time. Thank you again for looking over my résumé, and I hope that you will consider bringing me in for a more personal conversation. I relish the chance to discuss work opportunities with you, and I hope to hear from you soon.

Regards,

John Smith

Cold-Call Letters

These are letters where you are submitting an unsolicited résumé for review. You may intend to limit your job search to advertised positions and think this type of cover letter is unnecessary, and perhaps a little aggressive. But, the truth of the current economic times is that companies don't need to pay to advertise for applicants – the applicants are coming to them.

I recently sat in a city commission meeting as they amended their recruiting and hiring policy for this very reason. The city had an open position, and the old recruiting policies required that the city advertise that opening through paid advertisement. After receiving over 200 applications for that open position and noting the unemployment rate in the city was nearing ten percent, one of the commissioners decided free advertisement of open positions would suffice, and he presented his idea to the other commissioners. In a unanimous decision, that small city commission did what many companies around the country are doing – taking themselves off the market and waiting for job seekers to come to them.

In fact, the Professional Résumé Writers Association estimates between 75 and 80 percent of all employment opportunities are never posted. Since that is the case, there are a staggering amount of unadvertised job openings out there that you will never be in the running for if you do not pursue more aggressive means of getting your résumé circulated for consideration. The truth is, you will rarely hurt yourself by sending a résumé and cover letter to a company, even if it is unsolicited. The worst case scenario is they will simply discard your correspondence. Just remember:

You can never be told "yes" if you do not ask the question.

But you should not just sent your résumé out to various companies unsolicited without a means of introduction. The cold-call cover letter is the ideal way to extend your greeting to a potential employer. Within this category of cover letters, there are a few different audiences you might target, including the broadcast letter, networking letter, or referral letter.

The first letter in this category is the **broadcast letter**. This type of cover letter is used to "broadcast" or advertise your employment availability to a large audience of employers. You will use this letter to introduce yourself to your recipient and transmit your résumé to them in the absence of networking or referral. This may seem like a waste of time, but remember that figure of un-advertised job openings. If there is a company at which you have always wanted to work, why not give it a try?

Since the recipient of a broadcast letter will not know you, what you include in your letter is extremely important to the outcome of this type of job hunting process. Remember, these employers did not seek out your résumé by posting a job listing. They may not even be actively looking to hire. If you want interviews to come from this form of job search (and they will if done properly), you must spend some quality time assembling this type of cover letter.

The most important thing to remember when preparing a broadcast letter is this:

Never address your letter to the HR Department.

The human resource department is inundated with résumés, both from responses to advertisements and unsolicited ones. You do not want your résumé to sink in with the thousands of "kept on file" documents if you are using this approach.

It is vitally important that you **get personal**. It might be acceptable to use a "Dear Hiring Authority" greeting when submitting a cover letter and résumé to an advertised position, but if you are going to show a company you are really interested in working for them when they aren't even conducting a candidate search, you need to show real ingenuity.

Instead of sending your résumé and cover letter to the personnel director, find the appropriate manager for which you would like to work and address your letter to him/her. This may involve a bit of digging on your part, but it often only takes a few phone calls to get this information.

The second most important thing to remember when assembling a broadcast letter is that:

Research is Fundamental.

If you are conducting this sort of campaign, you must do more than just discover the name of the person you address your cover letter to. You must try to show genuine interest and enthusiasm for the company. The employer is not merely looking for another individual to "push buttons" to enter their ranks. They want someone who will be a dynamic, positive influence that will help them achieve success in their industry. Your letter must show that you not only know something about the company, but can convey which of your strengths can meet their current needs.

Another important aspect of research is understanding, when possible, the corporate culture of the company. Since your cover letter can convey your personality, it might be a good indicator to a hiring director of whether you fit in with their atmosphere. A company that is casual and relaxed might overlook a cover letter that sounds stiff. Conversely, a company that prizes formality might not consider a letter that reads as informal. Finding the "perfect fit" for companies is about more than finding the person with the right skills. They are looking for someone who will fit into the dynamic of their office. While you can't fit a square peg in a round hole, if you want to get as many interviews as possible, it might be best to present yourself as square when need be and round when the time calls.

There will be plenty of times when you won't be able to tell how to do this, but when you are sending out "cold call" letters and you have to do research anyway – go ahead and go the extra mile to see what you can discover about a company's corporate culture and tailor your résumé accordingly.

The second type of "cold-call" cover letter is the **networking letter.** It is designed for job seekers to send out to professional and private associates informing them of your career goals and asking if they can assist you or refer you to someone who can. The purpose of this letter is threefold:

1. Acquaint the contact with your qualifications – a personal contact may not be familiar with all of your professional skills.

2. Get your résumé out.

3. Accumulate a list of referrals to contact in your job search.

You may not think you have many people you can target with this type of letter, but the truth is that from students to stay-at-home moms ready to reenter the workforce, everyone has networking contacts. If you are shaking your head, not knowing whom to address this type of letter to, here are some examples to inspire you:

Professional networks: This includes coworkers, colleagues, supervisors, and managers from past and present employers. These are often the best resources in your effort to secure a job. These people are typically in the same industry that you are in, and can give firsthand accounts of the quality of your work.

Community networks: This includes business professionals from your local community, such as bankers, lawyers, real estate brokers, and small business owners whom you have a working relationship with (basically people outside of your company that you do business with).

Association networks: This includes members of professional and community associations, such as churches, alumni associations, or parent booster clubs.

College/University networks: This includes people you went to school with, current or former professors, and administrators.

Personal networks: This includes friends, family members, and neighbors.

Networking letters should be a more casual letter. You are writing to friends and associates asking for their assistance, not a job. The more successful way to write these letters is to approach them like you are asking for nothing more than your reader's advice. That way, they feel comfortable responding. If you ask them for more than they can give you, you will likely not get a positive response. Anyone can give advice, but not everyone has a job to give you.

A successful response will give you at least one of three things:

- A recommendation or referral for a specific employment opportunity

- Information about specific companies

- Additional contacts that you can add to your network

You may use similar cover letters for many of your networking contacts, but remember to personalize the opening of each one. You are writing to people you know, and you do not want them to feel like they received a form letter. Additionally, different networks will likely need slightly different approaches. For example, your work associates will probably know more about your skills than your personal contacts. You will need to tailor your letters to your audience.

In addition to maximizing your professional and personal networks, don't forget about online networks. Social networking Web sites like **MySpace.com** and **Facebook.com** offer some limited business networking opportunities, and they will certainly allow you to touch base with old colleagues and friends you may have lost track of who may serve to expand your traditional networks. However, in a February blog, Danny Huffman wrote about **LinkedIn.com**, drawing my attention to the business networking Web site for the first time. The Web site welcomes students through executive level professionals, allowing people from all stages on the career path to be "linked in."

LinkedIn works by allowing registered users to maintain a list of business contacts, called "connections." They can invite anyone to become a connection. That list can be used to build up your online network by connecting you with second and third degree connections (the connections of your connections, and so on). LinkedIn also allows employers to list jobs and search for potential candidates, while job seekers can see profiles of hiring managers and discover which of their current contacts might facilitate an introduction. This makes the networking and referral letter process much easier and is a resource that should not be overlooked.

The third type of letter in this category is the **referral letter.** You will use this type of cover letter to address your letter and résumé to someone who was suggested to you by a friend or colleague (these may follow the results you get from your networking letters). The purpose of the referral letter is similar to that of the networking letter:

1. Set the stage for a personal meeting.

2. Transmit your résumé.

3. Acquaint the contact with your qualifications in advance of your networking phone call or meeting.

The Referral Letter is a vital document when sending your résumé out this way. The chances of a hiring manager reading an unsolicited résumé from someone they do not know are not great. By connecting yourself with someone they are familiar with, you significantly increase the likelihood that your résumé will be given serious consideration. The key to the success of a referral letter is that the person doing the referring be immediately recognizable to the target audience. Otherwise, the impact of the referral is negated. Be sure to mention the referral upfront and draw an immediate connection to them in the mind of your reader, particularly if your reference is someone they know well, but from years ago.

If the referral letter is well written, it will make the person whom you are contacting feel comfortable. Hopefully comfortable enough to share information like job leads and names of contacts. It should also provide sufficient information about your qualifications and job-search objectives so that the contact can make quality recommendations to you and share information about you with others.

A referral letter requires you to do certain things other letters might not, so it is important to note them here. A well-written referral letter will include:

- A personalized opening paragraph where you name the person who referred you, state the nature of your relationship with that person, and pepper it with personal comments where appropriate.

- A brief summary of qualifications and a reference to an enclosed or attached résumé.

- An action statement designed to initiate the next step, like setting up a networking call or personal meeting. Remember, unlike a letter to a headhunter or in response to an advertised job opening, this reader does not benefit from meeting you. You should take the initiative.

- Statement of appreciation.

In addition to those elements, the referral letter may include any of the following:

- An explanation on how the referral came about.

- Reason for the job/career change (particularly if a move will be involved).

- Reference to a known job opening, if one exists.

- Personal comment from the person doing the referring.

Remember that just like the networking letter, every referral and résumé letter sent will not come back with a job prospect. But, the combination of the networking and referral letters is an ideal way to get your résumé out and find your ideal job.

Examples of "cold-call" letters are listed on the following pages:

Broadcast "cold-call" cover letter:

Harold "Harry" Williams   *hwilliams86@gmail.com*
7849 North Center Street   *Residence: (489) 555-9899*
West Bend, WI 58939   *Mobile: (478) 555-9878*

June 5, 2009
Ms. Susan Henderson
Executive Director of Sales
WidgetSalesRUs
78476 Widget Drive
Nonamesville, CA 97680

Dear Ms. Henderson:

I consider myself extremely fortunate to have come across an article in The Widget Gazette that states you will soon be expanding into West Bend. I have often found myself admiring the quality of your widgets, and have longed for the opportunity to join a company who strives to be a driving force in the widget industry.

I have just recently graduated from West Widget University with a major in Widgetry and a minor in Gadgetry. I know that your company has maintained a 57 percent market share for close to a decade now, providing widgets to both domestic and international consumers. I've learned that your breakthrough in compound widgeting — the science of melding two distinct widgets to form a brand new widget with properties of both parent widgets — has earned you several awards and distinctions, including the 2006 West Coast Widget Conference award. I know that being a recent graduate, I may lack the experience you seek, but I graduated magna cum widget and have a burning desire to explore all the opportunities that widgetry has to offer. I have participated in a number of studies involving the advancement of nanowidgetry and feel I can use my experience to help your company break into this new market segment. I have attached my résumé, which details the research and experience I have attained in this field

In conclusion, I believe that you will find that I am worthy of consideration for your new West Bend office. I believe I have the proper knowledge and experience to grow in an entry-level position and provide you valuable assets in achieving even greater success in the widget world. I look forward to meeting with you soon.

Regards,

Harold Williams

Referral "cold-call" cover letter:

JANICE WILLIAMS
121 East Bird Blvd.
Small Town WI 84932
(978) 555-8373
Jwilliams41868@email.com

September 7, 2009

Ms. Marsha Long
Vice President & General Counsel
Bradley, White and Jones
4783 Lincoln Ave.
Big Town WI 83272

Dear Ms. Long:

Ashley Grant, one of my colleagues at Swanson Inc., suggested that I contact you. I understand that you and Ashley began your careers together at Cheese America and worked together for over ten years. She speaks very highly of you.

Ms. Long, I am a corporate attorney and have worked in the legal division of Swanson Inc. for three years since my graduation from Yale Law School in 2006. My area of concentration has been Human Resource law, although I assisted colleagues in both patent and anti-trust cases.

I have attached a copy of my résumé for your reference.

My husband, Jack, and I have decided to relocate to Bigtown. Jack has been offered a wonderful career opportunity there that we feel would be a mistake for him to turn down. Therefore, I find myself searching for a position that will be a positive career move for me as well. Ashley was confident you would be able to assist me in my search.

Even if you do not know of any specific openings for someone with my credentials, I would like to meet with you when I am in town the first week of October. Ashley thought you might be able to introduce me to some of your colleagues as well to give me a jump-start on my networking goals in your community. Thank you for your assistance in this matter.

Sincerely,

Janice Williams

Online Cover Letters

The fourth category of cover letters is those you might attach to an online résumé. Monster, Yahoo Hotjobs, and other job sites will all allow you to upload and submit a résumé online for employers to review. They will ask if you would like to submit a cover letter along with that résumé. If you choose to put a cover letter online to introduce yourself, recognize several things.

More than likely, you will be addressing a recruiter, not a hiring director. Yet, you probably do not want to include all of the information you would when addressing a recruiter. For example, there is no need to put your geographical preferences and salary requirements in an online cover letter. You want to leave this particular introduction as basic as possible. And above all else, you do *not* want to use this saved cover letter when you submit your résumé online. You still want to tailor a cover letter for the specific position you are applying to.

The following example is ideal for this type of cover letter:

Trisha Smith
301 West Peach Tree St.
Atlanta, GA 48273
(797) 555-9484

Dear Sir/Ma'am:

After working 12 years for a small, family-run insurance company, I find myself looking for new employment. The wonderful owner passed away, and the family has decided not to continue the business he started. I worked as his bookkeeper and administrative assistant from the time I graduated with my bachelor's from the

University of Georgia until now.

While his passing is a great loss for me, it is with excitement that I embark on my quest for a new job. I am detail-oriented, keeping perfect books the entire time I worked at my current position (which held up to the close scrutiny of an IRS audit in 2002). I am excellent at multitasking, managing my duties as a mother of two boys and my employer's busy office schedule. I'm a self-starter who doesn't need to be asked to fill a need – I simply get things done.

My résumé is listed detailing my skills and accomplishments, but I would enjoy speaking with any interested parties in greater length about how I can assist their office like I did for so many years for my former employer.

Regards,

Trisha Smith

CHAPTER 3

The Handshake

Chapter two outlined three basic rules of cover letter writing, four types of cover letters to compose, and seven components each cover letter must include. This chapter, and the next two, will give a detailed look at the main content of your cover letter.

Imagine yourself at a social event, where there are dozens of guests mingling throughout the room. You spot a hiring manager for a company at which you would love to be employed. You work your way across the room and wait for a break in the conversation she is engaged in. Her head turns toward you; you greet her by name and extend your hand to introduce yourself. You have seconds to make an impression on her that will get you a business card or an invitation to e-mail your résumé.

The opening of your cover letter is like that handshake and brief introduction. Your reader is like that manager at a social event: busy, attention divided, not focused on you, and easily diverted.

Just like you will have to make a quick impression on that manager in the above example, your cover letter will be quickly dismissed if you don't make an immediate impact. According to

Danny Huffman of Career Services International, a hiring executive may spend as little as 15-18 seconds reading your cover letter before they decide if they want to continue reading or put your cover letter down.

"Your first paragraph must entice the reader with value and substance," said Huffman. The most important part of your cover letter is your first couple of sentences. Hiring authorities may peruse dozens of applications a day. Your cover letter is necessary to distinguish yourself from the crowd and it must do so quickly.

An opening paragraph with an impact will accomplish three tasks:

1.　Start with a unique first sentence.

2.　Introduce yourself to the reader.

3.　Tell the reader why you are writing the letter.

Most cover letters will accomplish two of these three tasks with a generic opener, like:

> *I am responding to the advertisement for a B2B sales director on* **hotjobs.com***. I have attached my résumé for your consideration.*

While using that as your opening sentence may not get your cover letter tossed, it is important to consider that your reader may have read that exact same line 20 times already by the time he gets around to reading yours.

At the same time, it is best not to go overboard with an opening line like:

*With ten years of experience in marketing, I am the answer to your company's needs! You can pull the advertisement for a marketing manager off **Monster.com** right now, because after you read my attached résumé, you will know you have found the right person for the job.*

Like your handshake, your opening paragraph should be neither too weak, like the first example, nor overbearing, like the second. When you write your opening paragraph, you may want to pose a question that focuses in on a high-need area for the employer, like:

Can you use a law enforcement officer with a case-closure rate of 90 percent to help decrease the crime rate in your city?

Just make sure the answer to whatever question you include in your opening paragraph is "yes." "Don't let your first paragraph give the reader a chance to think 'no'," said Huffman. Remember, this is your commercial. Don't let them flip that channel on you and switch over to someone else's cover letter. Consider the following suggestions to help you find the right "grip," if you will, to start you cover letter.

Start with a Unique Sentence

Remember, your goal is not to shock your reader, but simply to stand out from the crowd a little. If you are having trouble getting started, consider the following suggestions to help you construct a standout opening line(s):

- **Refer to a Prior Conversation.**

Of course, you can't do this if you have never spoken to the hiring authority; but if you have, you have a distinct advantage. This is an advantage that can come by researching the company or position for which you are applying.

Example:

We spoke on the phone Monday about the accounting position you have available. Per your request, I am forwarding you my résumé, which highlights ten years of accounting experience. I am confident you will find my skills well suited for the opening you need to fill.

This advantage may also be gained through networking. When writing a "cold-call" letter to someone you have a business contact or relationship with, you should mention that in your opening sentence.

Example:

I enjoyed coordinating with you last quarter on the Jameson Hall project. I was very impressed with the way your company conducts business and am interested in joining your amazing team of professionals.

• **Name Drop.**

People are more likely to read cover letters from applicants who are referred to them by a trusted friend or colleague. If you have a mutual contact with the hiring authority, don't expect them to realize that when they see your list of references. Tell them upfront.

Example:

At the recommendation of Donna Gates, I am contacting you to express my interest in the opening you have for an administrative assistant.

- **Lead with an accomplishment.**

When you don't have either of the aforementioned options available to you, it is best to give the reader a reason early on to read the rest of your cover letter and go on to review your résumé. Therefore, you might try listing an outstanding achievement in your opening line.

Example:

Under my leadership as State Coordinator for Tutoring Express in Alabama, the program expanded from 15 schools to 50, employing over 250 tutors that provide small-group instruction to over 3,000 students. Now that I have relocated to Georgia, I would like to speak with you about how I can provide those same results for your organization.

- **Show that you have done your homework.**

Another way to provide a unique start to your cover letter is by quoting the hiring authority directly or stating some statistic about the company and/or industry. This shows that you have done research about your target audience, the company, and the position for which you wish to be considered.

Example:

In a recent article for Newsweek, you were quoted as saying, "The best way to advertise your company is to turn your customers into your advertisers. We provide such phenomenal customer service that over 80 percent of our new business comes from referrals." When I read that, I knew that your company was the right one for my people skills and passion for giving my best to my customers.

I read in the Orlando Sentinel that your restaurant intends to open your first restaurant in Florida on International Drive near the theme parks. I have five years of experience as a hostess at two four-star dining facilities in that area. I am very interested in putting my knowledge and skills to work for you as your maître d'.

Introduce Yourself to the Reader

Tell your reader right from the start who you are and what you do for a living. That information may have been conveyed in your opening sentence(s), but if not, you should follow that introduction immediately with that information.

Introduction for an **advertised job opening:**

As an assistant manager with a very successful retail company, I have been a leader of a high-performing sales team that exceeds targeted goals on a regular basis.

I have ten years of experience as a certified public accountant and am responding to your advertisement for an executive accountant.

Introduction to a **headhunter/recruiting agency:**

> *As an employment agency specializing in the recruitment of administrative talent, you may be interested in my years of experience as an administrative assistant and executive assistant.*

Introduction for a **"cold-call" letter:**

> *It was with great interest that I read of your company's pending expansion to the East Coast. As an award-winning chef in Baltimore, my talents and years of experience would benefit you greatly as you prepare to open new locations in my area.*

Tell the Reader Why You are Writing the Letter

In all honesty, your reader knows why you are writing this letter. No matter what type of cover letter you are addressing, if you have sent a cover letter and résumé, you are inquiring about a job opening. Still, it is best to state this plainly and be very specific as to which job opening you are inquiring about.

Being specific will help a human resource office ensure that your cover letter and résumé gets read by the right person. For example, if you are applying for a marketing position, it will not do you any good for the information technology manager to read your résumé and cover letter. It will help a recruiter match your résumé up with the right employment opportunities. It will even help the recipient of a broadcast letter better focus on what opportunities they might have available to you.

This will likely be the final line of your opening paragraph, and citing a specific job advertisement, job opening, or position is a good way to transition into the second paragraph of your cover letter, where you detail why you are right for the job and/or company.

Example for an **advertised job opening:**

> *I am writing in response to the posting for a sports reporter listed on www.jobwebsite.com.*
>
> *I would like my résumé to be considered for the position of technical writer that was advertised on www.jobwebsite.com.*

Example for a **headhunter/recruiting agency:**

> *I am relocating to Atlanta and believe my qualifications would be well suited for one of your clients. I have attached my résumé for your review.*
>
> *I am aware that you recruit for businesses within my area of expertise. I am looking for a new career challenge and have attached my résumé for your consideration.*

Example for a **"cold-call" cover letter:**

> *I have followed your company with great interest as you have expanded into my area of the country. Now that you are opening a location in my home town, I would like to submit my résumé for your consideration. I believe you will find my qualifications well suited for your company.*

The examples I have listed may seem to overlap information; therefore, consider the following examples as they assemble these three elements together for complete opening paragraphs:

Opening paragraph for an **advertised job opening:**

> *Capturing a ninety-mile-an-hour fast pitch on film is no easy task, but that is the kind of challenging work I excel in as a professional photographer. My extensive and varied background in sports/motion capture imaging makes me an excellent candidate to fill the advertised opening for a **lead photographer***.*

Opening paragraph for a **headhunter/recruiting agency:**

> *I sell something that no one wants to admit they need – I sell life insurance. And I do it extraordinarily well with a customer satisfaction rating of 94 percent. If I can serve my customers that well, think of how well my sales expertise can fill the needs of your clientele that are looking for proven sales managers. I am submitting my résumé for your consideration in your recruiting efforts.*

Opening paragraph for a **"Cold-call" letter:**

> *When so many parts of the country are facing tough economic times, it is exciting to be part of a growing community like Clarksville. An expanding public works department is a natural extension of that growth. I learned about an opening in that department from my long-time friend Rod Smith, and per his recommendation, I am forwarding my résumé to you.*

*Bolding the job title you are applying to can prove helpful to human resource personnel who are looking to place your cover letter and résumé with the appropriate hiring manager. This is particularly important when the advertisement you are responding to does not mention a specific job identification number.

CHAPTER 4

The Sales Pitch

Chapter three delved into the first paragraph of your cover letter, where you introduce yourself to your potential employer. The next section of your cover letter is your sales pitch. This is where you convince your reader that they need to give you an interview and get to know you better. This is where you sell yourself as the answer to their employment needs. In this chapter, we will examine how to present yourself in the best light possible to your audience.

The Value of Honesty

First and foremost: be honest. There may be times when someone like a graduating student or a stay-at-home parent returning to the work force looks to "fluff" up their cover letter and résumé, but you should never exaggerate or falsify information in your cover letter and résumé. The hiring director may never discover your deceit, but if they do, you have permanently disqualified yourself with that person and anyone they may talk to about you. Additionally, if the deceit is discovered after you have been hired, it may be grounds for dismissal. Honesty is simply the best policy.

That said, even with "truth in advertising" laws, companies project themselves in the best possible light. You too should put the most positive spin on your accomplishments and experience as possible. Be sure to highlight any noteworthy achievements or accomplishments. For example, if you're an accountant who managed to catch a billing error that saved your company millions of dollars, advertise it. After all, most companies are looking to hire the best possible candidates, not the ones who just "get the job done."

In the body of your cover letter (which may span one to three paragraphs), you will want to accomplish the following:

- Comment on your knowledge of the company and why you are interested in working for them, if you did not include information like this in your opening.

- Acknowledge the skills required for the job opening, as described in the job listing, if there is one.

- Discuss the skills and strengths you bring to the job, striking parallels to the needs of the position.

- Briefly describe a related achievement or success story and how it will transfer to the job for which you are applying.

- State how you think you and the company would be a good fit.

In preparing this section of your cover letter, you will want to take your résumé in hand and carefully examine it. You will need to make careful note of all the requirements and wish lists in the job posting and try to cross reference those to your work experience and skill sets. You will want to highlight anything that seemingly addresses a need that the prospective employer has, and you will do this in the "sales pitch" portion of your cover letter. You should also emphasize any unique skills or accomplishments from your résumé in your sales pitch. Often, HR personnel will consider a person for other jobs, even if the cover letter was not written specifically for those positions. Emphasizing your strengths may open other doors you were not previously aware of.

What you include in your sales pitch may differ from one job application to another. However, there is one basic strategy when writing this part of your cover letter – **STAR** it.

Fill Your Cover Letter with STARs.

STAR stands for **Statement, Task, Action**, and **Result**. It is not enough to list your qualifications; you must make your reader believe these things about you. "Remember, it is not sufficient to simply create a list of specific skills — words without confirmation are meaningless," said Danny Huffman of Career Services International. "Statistics indicate people tend to believe approximately seven percent of what is 'told' and 93 percent of what is shown. Given these numbers, theory without practice can be damaging."

In other words, "I'm a great salesperson" doesn't mean much to your reader. But, "As a member of a 50-person sales team, I was the lead salesperson for 11 of the 14 quarters for which I was employed," is a much better indicator of your sales skills.

STAR breaks down as follows:

Statement: this will be the qualification for the job that you wish to highlight.

Task: This should be an example of something you did that showcases the statement you made. Do you have great bookkeeping skills? Then list a task you performed as a bookkeeper.

Action: This is the action you took to perform that task. How did you perform the task you choose to showcase? What were the steps you took to accomplish that task?

Result: This is a great way to show a hiring director what they can expect to see if they choose you for a position. What was the result of that action you performed? Did sales go up? Did the company expand? Did the company win an award?

Now that you understand the basic format for writing your sales pitch, how do you select which elements of your résumé to discuss in your cover letter? Start by putting yourself in the shoes of your reader. Pretend you are scheduling interviews for the position or positions you have posted. What would capture your interest? What would make you pause and look at a particular applicant's cover letter and résumé? Let's start with the following selling points:

- **Making money**: Do you have a proven track record for generating income, increasing sales, or bringing in new customers? Non-profit organizations aside, businesses have one main purpose: to make money. Highlight any accomplishments or skills that show you have experience in making or helping others make money. Don't neglect volunteer work when preparing your cover letter. Any skill that can generate revenue will be welcomed, regardless of how you acquired it. For example, years of experience in fund-raising can be used to show your potential employer that you will be a great money maker.

- **Saving money**: Did you help reduce costs in previous positions? Did you head up a streamlining project that eliminated unnecessary expenditures? Even a stay-at-home mom who is returning to the work force can discuss household budgeting skills and how she opened college funds for her children with the money she was able to save in other expenses.

- **Being innovative**: Have you created new products, processes, courses, or companies? Don't underestimate the value of showing off your creative side. Maybe you created a specialty drink while working as a bartender or created an employee training guide. It is possible to take what you think are small accomplishments and use them to demonstrate the skills your potential employer requires.

- **Making improvements**: Did you take an inefficient system and make it work better? Were you instrumental at improving quarterly sales? Most companies will not need you to recreate the wheel when you join their team. So, as important as being innovative is, a proven track record at improvement will show your potential employer exactly why you would be a valuable asset.

- **Leadership**: Did you lead, or were you part of any teams that accomplished significant goals in the company? Leadership skills, as well as the ability to work as part of a team, are often at the top of the list of desirable attributes for many job applicants. Be sure to include any examples of these in your cover letter.

- **Achievements, honors, and awards**: You don't want to create the "My child was honor student of the week at Roosevelt Preschool," effect in your cover letter, so if your company gives out trophies like candy, select the most prestigious ones to include. Otherwise, consider all honors you have received when putting together your cover letter, particularly if you are a recent graduate or returning to the job force after taking time off. Sports or charity awards may demonstrate the skills your potential employer desires even if your work history does not.

After examining your résumé closely with these questions in mind, you may now have a very long list of items to include in your cover letter. But, as we have established, your cover letter needs to be compact, concise, and needs to make an impact. How can you accomplish this?

The body of your cover letter will be tailored according to the type of cover letter you are writing and the company/person to whom you are addressing your letter. What you include from the list you assembled may differ from cover letter to cover letter. When you are writing a cover letter in response to an advertised position, you will have the easiest time selecting which skills and achievements to highlight because you will want to match your abilities up to that company's needs.

The trick is to read the job posting carefully, make note of the requirements, and try to address those requirements in the letter. For example, the posting might require that all applicants have at least five years of experience in sales. Make sure to note that you meet or exceed those criteria in the cover letter. Sometimes that list of requirements can be fairly lengthy in and of itself. So, how can you possibly address all those requirements in a half-page paragraph? This gets a bit trickier.

I would suggest picking three to five of the most important "requirements" and addressing those. For example, a job posting will often ask you to have X number years of experience at a position. I would consider this as an important requirement; a "first tier" requirement if you will. Another requirement might be that you have some experience in graphics design. If it doesn't explicitly ask for a quantitative measure of your experience (such as how many years you've done this particular job), I would put this into a secondary importance tier. If you have space to address it, do so, but make sure you address first-tier requirements before you touch on the secondary tier requirements.

When you are writing a cover letter to a recruiting agency or a "cold-call" letter to a company expressing your interest in working for them, you will have to do some research to decide what to include. Typically, these types of cover letters should highlight your most important skills or greatest experience in the broadest range possible. Additionally, they should also reflect your most recent experience. For example, you may have designed Web sites ten years ago while the Internet was in its fledgling state, but if you haven't done any related work since then, leave this information out of your cover letter.

Database Creation

Customizing each cover letter can be a time consuming process. However, you will find shortcuts in the process. The biggest shortcut I can suggest is to create a database of all your skills and achievements (preferably in the STAR format) so that you can cut and paste them into your cover letter according to the needs of the letter you are writing.

To accomplish this database, follow these easy steps:

Step one: Select the skills, accomplishments, and honors you wish to highlight. Create the most extensive list you can compile. Do not omit anything you may see as trivial. You may not assign that particular skill or accomplishment much weight, but you never know when it might be useful at some future job listing.

Step two: Take your selections and write about them as both bulleted items and in story-telling form so you can use them in either type of cover letter format. Remember to follow the STAR guideline as much as possible — make a **S**tatement, talk about a **T**ask that you performed that demonstrates your statement, describe the **A**ction you took to perform that task, and share the **R**esults of your action.

Step three: Revamp the simple sentences you have created into dynamic ones using the recommendations detailed in chapter eight.

Step four: Organize these selections in a way that makes sense to you (you might create categories by positions held, by types of skills, or by most-to-least important for example) and save them in a document so that when you are compiling your individual cover letters, you can cut and paste from your database into your personalized cover letter. This will save you both time and effort, while making your cover letters more personal and unique.

Once you have your database of accomplishments to include in the body of any cover letter you write, you will need to decide which items to cut and paste. In doing that, consider the following questions:

- Which of my skill sets best match the advertised requirements?

- Which of my skills sets are most useful to this company?

- Which of my skills sets make me stand out the most?

- Which of my skills sets differentiate me from my competition?

After you have selected which accomplishments and experience you wish to take from your résumé and highlight in your cover letter, consider the following recommendations as well:

Rephrase

While your cover letter is a complementary document to your résumé, it should not be a summation of it. So, avoid using the copy-and-paste button when picking points of your résumé to put in your cover letter. You will need to summarize that information, not repeat it verbatim.

Additionally, your résumé is often tailored to impress the manager you would be working under. Unfortunately, they are usually not the first person to read your cover letter. So while cutting and pasting some job-related jargon might impress the manager, the HR personnel might not necessarily have a clue what you are talking about. You want to be accurate and informative in your cover letter, but you don't want to be obtuse. Remember, you are trying to get past the "weed out" process and onto an interview. The weeding out is usually done by the hiring director, who often has a list of "buzzwords" the hiring manager wants them to look for, so you will definitely want those in your résumé — but do not overwhelm them with too much jargon.

Another advantage of creating that database of skills and accomplishments is that you will have already done this, and you will not have to worry about cutting and pasting from your résumé in a hurry.

Personalize

There is room in your cover letter to put personal information in that might be excluded from a résumé. For example, if you have roots in a community or a connection to an organization, you may want to mention that in this sales pitch paragraph.

Example:

I am a highly energetic and innovative sales person with over 15 years of experience in business to business sales. I have consistently exceeded sales objectives and increased revenue where I have been employed.

My achievements are due to my ability to create and maintain rapport with the individuals within the organization to which I belong — be it professional or personal. That skill coupled with a drive to provide exceptional customer service has led me to be recognized seven times by the Chamber of Commerce for excellence is salesmanship.

My wealth of contacts and deep roots in the community would greatly aide your company as it expands into this state. Those contacts include, but are not limited to:

Add On

In chapter one, you were advised to ensure that your résumé and cover letter complemented each other. Generally speaking, you should not include information in your cover letter that is not in your résumé, but there are some exceptions to that rule.

For example, if you are applying for a store management position at a large retail store and have years of sales and management experience, but have not worked in retail since you were in college (therefore, the position is too old to have as part of your work history), you may want to note that in the following way:

Years ago, my first job in a retail sales position, where I worked my way up to assistant manager while obtaining my bachelor's degree in finance, allowed me to be mentored under one of the best general managers I have ever encountered. That experience taught me a great deal about being a manager in general, and I have never forgotten the proven sales techniques I learned in that retail position.

With these guidelines in mind, consider the following examples of content paragraphs for each type of cover letter:

The Solicited Response:

The advertisement:

> *SYSTEM ADMINISTRATOR – Democratic Senator is seeking a systems administrator for a fast-paced office. Responsibilities include updating and maintaining network hardware and software, developing and maintaining an information management system for the office, maintaining computer security, and providing computer assistance and training as needed. Individual must be well-organized, detail-oriented, and able to work independently. Experience with Web site maintenance and content management is a plus. A bachelor's degree in computer engineering is highly desired. Position is based in D.C.* **Please e-mail cover letter and résumé to senateemployment@email.com and include reference number in the subject line.**

Response:

> *I currently administer the Web site and forum: www.website.com as a medium through which those on the "Hill" can communicate to every day citizens. My experience in that position and my former position as the system administrator for Senator Smith make me well qualified for this position. My qualifications include:*
>
> - *Building and maintaining a five-server network in the Senator's office that included an e-mail server, an SQL database server, and several file system servers that housed much of the office's sensitive materials.*
>
> - *Building and maintaining most of the office's desktop and laptop computers, as well as managing the software content on all of those machines.*

- *Creating the office's safe usage standard, which included anti-virus and ad-ware programs, to minimize downtimes for office machines.*

- *Training the entire office personnel on all the software that was installed on their machines, and being responsible for upgrading that software and retraining the office on any new features that may have been added.*

- *Site layout and design, including setting up the PHPBoard forums and providing security for all the forum moderators.*

Additionally, I have extensive experience with Quorum, as I have worked for several congressional offices prior to my last one. I have also helped the former Senator create and maintain a blog so he can best reach out to his constituency. He feels this alone has helped him remain grounded and focused on the main reason he went into politics: to look after the interests of the people.

Letters to a Headhunter or Recruiter:

I have been in the technology industry for over 15 years. I have a bachelor's degree in Computer Information Systems, and have recently held a product manager position at ABC software. I would be a valuable asset to any team. My strong qualifications are as follows:

- *An extensive background in web application development, with experiences in both Java and Visual Basic.*

- *Over ten years of experience in project management which emphasized initializing, guiding, and completing dozens software development projects.*

- *Experience as a photographer and graphic designer with certifications and publications in both areas of specialty.*

My latest achievement involved designing a subway kiosk system where passengers could enter information into regarding the best routes to their destination. I led a team of four programmers, one software architect, and two quality assurance engineers. Through our efforts, we were able to secure a 2.8 million dollar contract with the New York transit authority to implement and maintain this subway system near the Manhattan section of the New York subway.

On the creative side, my crowning achievement is my contribution to several recording artists' Web sites, most notably Dave Matthews Band's current Web site logo. I love the ability to merge my creative passions with the digital medium, and I feel I can offer a unique set of skills to many of your clients.

Cold-Call Letters:

In my years of experience, I have acquired a broad-based understanding of financial/banking needs at all levels of business. I am skilled in account management, sales management, customer service, marketing, branch management, loan administration, regulatory compliance, quality control, and teller operations. Throughout my career, I received recognition by management as a top performer for consistently achieving targeted sales goals and leading projects that have delivered profitable results and generated new business.

As a proven leader with excellent communication skills, I am proficient at motivating and training teams of professionals in meeting or exceeding identified company goals and customer expecta-

tions. With a proven track record of bringing in new customers and retaining existing accounts, I demonstrate excellent customer service and relationship building skills.

Online cover letters:

My years in the newspaper industry include six years I spent as the publisher and editor of my own community weekly in Alabama. The paper was established in the early 1900s, but by 1996 when I purchased the company, it was in a distressed condition, both in coverage and business operations. Under my leadership, we turned the situation around and I sold the paper in 2002 for 50 percent above the purchase price.

Prior to that, I worked eight years as the top editor and manager of a news department in Mobile. My column was widely read, and the paper increased its circulation by 25 percent during my time there. I trained the reporters that worked under me with diligence and high standards. Three of them now manage news rooms themselves for newspapers with circulations over 150,000.

After selling the weekly in 2002 and moving to Atlanta, I began a teaching career at the Peach Tree Charter High School in their remarkable journalism program. It has been my pleasure to be the faculty advisor for the student-run newspaper and guide these budding writers in all aspects of AP Style, sports reporting, and editing. However, now that my youngest child has graduated high school, I find myself longing again for the newsroom.

I have substantial experience with daily, semi-weekly, and weekly newspapers and total-market-coverage shopper publications as my posted résumé will further detail. I am an enthusiastic leader with substantial training and teaching experience. I am a cool-headed, conscientious builder and pride myself on being an effective motivator and problem-solver. I have spent years adapting quickly to an ever-changing business, and I work diligently to get the job done right.

My newsroom philosophy is: A newspaper should be satisfied with nothing less than the constant improvement of itself and the community it serves.

CHAPTER 5

The Closing

Chapter three helped you compile your introduction to your potential employer. In chapter four, you assembled your sales pitch to convince the employer that they need to get to know you better. In this chapter, you will learn how to close your cover letter. In that closing paragraph, you will want to convey some or all of the following:

- Restate any important themes, creatively tying them into a cohesive, emphatic final statement.

- Address personal or salary information if requested (you might mention willingness to relocate or travel if that information was requested or if you are addressing a head-hunter).

- Thank your reader for their time and consideration.

- Make a closing statement that indicates a call for action. Indicate your enthusiasm to hear from the hiring authority in order to schedule an interview. When it is appropriate, you may also state your intention to follow up with a personal phone call later.

The rest of the chapter will discuss the information you might want to include in your closing paragraph and give you examples of how to do it.

Salary Information

Salary information is usually a tough subject for people to address in their cover letters, and, generally speaking, it is never advantageous to volunteer salary information. Therefore, the main reason you would include this information is if it was specifically requested of you. There are two pieces of salary information that you may need to address: salary history and salary requirements.

When a potential employer asks you to provide this information, they are creating a potential screen in considering you for the position. Additionally, providing this information puts you at a disadvantage later in negotiations. But, it is sometimes required; if not in your cover letter, then later in the interview process. Here are some ways you may choose to address salary history, if you must:

- You may include a salary range. "My salary history has ranged from $60,000 to $70,000 in the past five years." This gives a glimpse of your salary history and fits well into the compactness of a cover letter. It also does not limit you to a specific number, and will give you some negotiating leeway if you are hired.

- If you choose to do so, you can provide specific information in the following format:

My salary history is as follows: Office manager ($30,000/year); Administrative assistant ($36,000/year); Executive assistant ($38,000); Executive office manager ($42,000/year).

In this example, you have briefly described your salary history while conveying a steady growth in income.

- You can prepare a separate page titled Salary History and include it as an enclosure.

- If the advertisement merely requests salary history, without explicitly stating that not providing it will eliminate you from consideration, you can choose not to discuss this information. However, since the request has been made, it is best to address the issue with a statement like, "I look forward to interviewing with you and will gladly provide you with a detailed salary history and my salary requirements at that time."

The other piece of salary information that may be requested in connection with salary history or by itself is your salary requirements. Once again, you may not want to confine yourself to a specific salary range when you enter negotiations later. But there may be times when this information is important — like when a recruiter requests this information to help him/her better match you up to clients.

Much like salary history, you have several options for answering this question:

- Go with a salary range that is general enough for a recruiter to match you with their clients or for a hiring authority to know whether you are in the ballpark for their budget. You can phrase the statement something like this: "My salary requirements are in the $55,000 to $65,000 range."

- You can give them a specific number: "My salary requirements are $70,000." However, this can hurt you in several ways. It can eliminate you from consideration for a position you would have accepted at a lower value, or it can hurt you in negotiations later if the company would have been willing to pay more.

- You can simply state that your salary requirements are negotiable. This is essentially avoiding the question, and while it might keep you in consideration, it might not be the best strategy to implement. You do know the base salary you need to accept to pay your bills, put food on your table, and meet other obligations. You probably want to make more than the base salary you need to survive, but it is not advisable for you to apply to positions that would pay you less than your monthly bills. Therefore, it might not be a bad idea to at least provide a salary range, particularly when you are addressing your cover letter to a headhunter.

- You can ignore the question entirely, but you will have to at least provide a salary range when dealing with a headhunter or a recruiter. They make their living finding the right candidate for their clients. They will not screen you onto the next stage of consideration if they do not think you will match their clients' needs.

Personal Information

This is information you might provide more to a headhunter or recruiting agency, but there are times when an advertisement might ask you about your willingness to relocate or travel. The following examples show you how to include that information in your closing paragraph:

Recruiter samples:

If you are working with a client company seeking a candidate with my qualifications, I would welcome the opportunity to be considered. Please be advised that my current compensation is $85,000 and I am open to relocation within the state of Florida. Thank you for your time. I look forward to hearing from you soon.

If you believe my qualifications are a good match for your current clientele, I would greatly appreciate the opportunity to speak with you further. To aid you in matching my information with your clients' needs, please be advised that I am willing to travel during the week and will consider relocating anywhere in the Southeast. My desired salary range is $75,000-$85,000. Thank you for your time. I look forward to speaking with you soon.

Ad-response samples:

I think you'll agree that I am an excellent candidate for this position. I am willing to relocate for an exciting and challenging opportunity and I believe the position with your company is exactly that. I would appreciate the opportunity to meet with you in person at your earliest convenience and will follow up with you by phone in that regard in a few days. Thank you.

I would welcome the chance to meet with you and discuss the international sales opportunities. On a personal note, I am single and rent my home, so relocation could be immediate. Thank you for your consideration.

Be Courteous

As you can see in the above examples, thanking your reader for their time is important. A recruiter, human resource director, or hiring authority will examine hundreds — if not thousands — of cover letters in a week. Gratitude, coupled with sincerity, will often leave a lasting impression with your reader. You want them to get to know you, and one of the best ways to do that is to be polite and courteous.

Call for Action

When you are making your closing statement, you want to express enthusiasm at the opportunity to continue in the consideration process. Do not present an excellent case for your qualifications as a candidate only to conclude with something like:

If you think I am the best qualified candidate for this position, please contact me at your earliest convenience.

In your closing paragraph you want to include a **call for action**. This means you will ask the letter recipient to take action, like scheduling an interview, or you volunteer to take action yourself.

Consider the following closing:

> *I am confident I can make a meaningful contribution as a sales associate for your company. I look forward to meeting with you to discuss further the details of this position and how I can improve your company's revenue. I will follow up with you in a few days to schedule an interview. Thank you very much for your consideration. I look forward to speaking with you soon.*

Note that in the second example, the writer states that they will follow up to schedule an interview with the reader. This is considered an aggressive closing, but sometimes it pays to be aggressive. Applicants who call a hiring authority to schedule an interview will have a better chance of getting one than those who don't.

However, that option is not always open to you, particularly when you are applying to an advertised position. In those cases, you can still make a strong closing with a statement like:

> *These qualities, along with others detailed in my résumé, make me an ideal candidate for this position. I would enjoy meeting with you to further discuss how I can make an immediate positive contribution to your company. Thank you for your time and consideration, and I look forward to hearing from you to schedule an interview at your earliest convenience.*

Just remember that your closing statement is a call to action. So if the action you want taken is the scheduling of an interview, don't be afraid to ask for it.

PART TWO

PACKAGING

CHAPTER 6

Formatting and Design

The formatting and design of your cover should convey professionalism and make you stand out. A well-designed cover letter is a great way to show that you have good computer skills. However, don't get carried away. It is unlikely your readers want to strain their eyes when reading your cover letter or **BE KNOCKED OUT OF THEIR SEAT WHEN THEY FIRST SET EYES ON IT**. There is a time and place *to get fancy with your font settings*, but your cover letter and résumé are not it.

Additionally, you do not want your cover letter to be overly designed with too much to distract the eye from the simple message you are trying to transmit: I am a great candidate — interview me.

Therefore, it is best to choose a simple yet sophisticated layout. You want your cover letter and résumé looking good without looking gaudy. If you are scratching your head, don't worry. This chapter will make recommendations on how to achieve that, and the final chapters of this book are full of appealing, professional sample cover letters for you to duplicate.

First off, there are a few typesetting rules you should follow:

- Only use one space after a period (instead of the two you were taught when you learned to type).

- Avoid underlining. If you wish to create a border above or below a line of text, such as a heading, use the "borders" or "paragraph rules" feature of your word processing program. If you wish to emphasize a specific point, using bold characters will be better than underlining.

- Double-space between paragraphs. Add a blank line of space after the date at the top and before your typed name at the bottom of your letter (i.e., your signature).

- Use a colon, not a comma, after your salutation.

Font

As mentioned before, it is best to use the same font in both your cover letter and your résumé. There are other ways to make a particular sentence or item stand out other than changing your font style.

Commonly used fonts include:

Tahoma	Verdana
Arial	Bookman Old Style
Times New Roman	Calibri

All of these fonts are included in the most recent version of Microsoft Office or have equivalents in other word processing applications. Avoid using customized or third-party fonts. They may look fantastic on your computer, but if the recipient's computer does not have that same font installed, the computer will make a "best guess" at the font, and that could lead to disastrous results in terms of how your résumé formatting will look. Therefore, be sure that when you e-mail your cover letter, it will translate well when your reader opens your document.

All of the above fonts were typed in the same font size. As you can see, they each vary in how much room they actually take up. You may remember from your days of writing essays in high school or college that various fonts allowed you to better fit your paper into the minimum/maximum range you were given. After all, who hasn't changed their font to something that will fill up pages quicker when writing a high school essay? I'm a professional writer, and I can still remember doing it. Well, now you can do the reverse. If you are finding it hard to fit all of your information in the cover letter on one page, you might want to consider using a small font type. Just don't go too small. Your cover letter has to remain legible.

Generally speaking, it is best to use a font size between 10 and 12, depending on the font type you have selected. If you stay within that range, your cover letter should appear very readable.

Paragraph Format

The two common ways you can format your paragraphs are to use a block format or an indented-paragraph format. Both are acceptable, and your decision will likely come down to your personal preference.

In the block format, every element of the letter is flush with the left margin, including the date, signature lines, and opening lines of each new paragraph.

In the indented-paragraph format, the date and signature lines will be indented four inches from the left margin, and the opening line of each paragraph will be indented one-quarter inch or one-half inch, depending on what you select.

Examples of each format are shown on the following pages:

Indented Paragraph Format:

Gordan R. "Robert" Jones

7849 North Center Street   *Residence: (489) 555-9899*
West Bend, WI 58939   *Mobile: (478) 555-9878*

December 1, 2009

Dear Hiring Authority:

I appreciate that you are taking the time to peruse my letter and résumé. I am writing in response to the job opening you have posted on the Senate job Web site regarding a systems administrator for a Democratic Senator. I believe that I have the right mixture of technical skills, Capitol Hill experience, and team-oriented personality to be an asset to your office.

I currently administer the Web site and forum: www.website. com as a medium through which those on the "Hill" can communicate to everyday citizens. I have done everything on this site, including designing the layout and graphics, setting up the PH-PBoard forums, and providing all the security for the forum moderators.

My other experience includes time spent as the systems administrator for Senator Jack Smith. In that position, I built and maintained a five-server network in the Senator's office that included an e-mail server, an SQL database server, and several file system servers that housed much of the office's sensitive materials. Additionally, I built and maintained most of the office's desktop and laptop computers, as well as managed the software content on all of those machines. I was also responsible for creating the office's safe usage standard, which included anti-virus and ad-ware programs, to minimize downtime of office machines.

Prior to that position, I worked for Congressman Dave Dullaney as the assistant systems administrator. In that position, I maintained all of the "back-end" systems, and was responsible for training the entire office personnel on all the software that was installed on their machines, including software upgrades I regularly maintained.

As you can see, I feel I have the necessary background and experience to meet the requirements for the job. I look forward to meeting you in person so that we may discuss whether I would be a good fit for the Senator's office. Thank you very much for taking the time to read this letter and look over my résumé. I hope to speak to you soon.

Regards,

Robert Jones

Block Paragraph Format:

Steve W "Will" Robinson

7849 North Center Street   *Residence: (489) 555-9899*
West Bend, WI 58939   *Mobile: (478) 555-9878*

Feb. 5th, 2009

Ms. Janie Brown
Atlantic Industries
jbrown@email.com

Dear Ms. Brown:

*I learned about your **Office Assistant** position through my job search on website.com. I am currently working as a customer service manager for an online paper supply company, but there is no room for advancement in this company at this time, so I am looking to branch out. I have attached my résumé for your review, as my skills appear to be a great match for your job opening.*

In my five years of employment with my current company, I assisted the owner significantly by handling all aspects of customer support and sales. One of my most rewarding experiences was when a large shipment to one of our customers failed to arrive on time. While it was not fun to deal with an understandably irate customer, it was my pleasure to track down their order and contact the shipping company to ensure that the customer received their order first thing the next day, which was in time for what they needed. I received a thank you letter from that manager for my diligence in customer service.

I am motivated by a drive to be excellent and a desire to see the company that I am working for prosper. I enjoy working in an office and performing administrative duties. I follow instructions to the letter, and I work late if a task needs extra effort to complete. Additionally, I am proficient in all Microsoft Office software, including Word, Excel, and PowerPoint.

I appreciate your time and consideration. I hope to meet with you to further discuss how I can be a valuable member of your team.

Sincerely,

Will Robinson

Bullets

Using bullets in the body of your cover letter makes it more readable. It is an excellent way to grab the attention of your reader and lead them to points you want them to read. A hiring director's eyes are immediately drawn to the bullet points and they get the essence of your message, even if they are just giving your cover letter a quick scan.

The bullet point format functions exceedingly well for two types of messages. It allows you to list your skills and accomplishments for your reader, which is particularly important if you are addressing your letter to a headhunter or conducting a cold-call letter to a company.

Example:

If any of your clients would benefit from my 15 years of lab management experience, I would enjoy the opportunity to work with you. My attached résumé details my achievements in streamlining business processes, maintaining quality control, and governing production and testing in a lab environment.

The core of my experience stems from an analytical perspective — concentration testing, flow-to-background testing, durability testing, and sensitivity testing while managing teams that were both creative and talented to produce highly focused yet technology-driven labs.

As a manager, I was exceptionally rated with a talent for improving work through monitoring quality performance. I also understand that to build up a solid team you must do it through sound operational processes and well-maintained logistics and procurement.

Evidence of my contributions can be seen through my success in:

- Managing the daily operations of a lab that manufactures non-destructive testing materials as dictated by military specifications. Our government contracts were fulfilled ahead of schedule and below budget, which is why we were awarded a new one every fiscal year.

- Overseeing several departments, including research and development, where I participated in over ten research projects that later led to successful company patents.

- Continual monitoring of employee performance with a deep commitment to process and productivity, which improved consistently every year under my leadership at each lab I ran.

With my scientific degrees, I am looking to transition into senior-level laboratory management. If you have any clientele that have such an opening, I hope you will recommend me for that position. Please be advised that my target salary range is $60,000-$70,000. I am willing to travel, but cannot consider relocation at this time. I realize it is important to get a feel for a person and believe a face-to-face meeting would be the best way for you to do that with me. I will contact you shortly to schedule a time that is convenient for us to meet.

This format also allows you to go point-by-point when responding to an advertised position showing how your experience meets their requirements. Consider the example on the following page:

Example:

*While browsing the current issue of Legal Briefs, I noticed your advertisement for a **Patent Attorney**. I interned for a pharmaceutical company while obtaining my B.S. in chemistry and continue to take great interest in the industry today. My attached résumé will demonstrate my knowledge of your industry and my experience as a patent attorney.*

I meet your specified requirements in the following ways:

- *I graduated magnum cum laude in my undergraduate degree from the University of Virginia. My legal degree is from Georgetown University.*

- *I currently work for a Widget USA — a small part manufacturing company — as their principal attorney in the patent area.*

- *In my five years of employment, I wrote over 50 patent applications for parts they developed, 30 of which were approved.*

- *During that same time, I successfully defended their patents in court ten times.*

I followed the Stephan Smith case that your company lost last September and gave serious consideration to what I would have done differently. I would like to share my thoughts with you on that subject as a demonstration of how my skills will meet your need for a creative, talented patent attorney. I look forward to scheduling a meeting with you at your earliest convenience.

In a variation of the bullet point format, some readers may choose to use a comparison chart, where you list their requirements and your qualifications side-by-side. Consider the example on the following page:

Example:

While the enclosed résumé illustrates more fully how my background is suited to your needs, please allow me to highlight the specific qualifications that meet your listed requirements:

Your Requirements:	My Qualifications:
• Bachelor's degree plus 3-5 years of marketing experience – preferably for a consumer packaged goods/retail company.	• I obtained bachelor's degrees in marketing and finance from Penn State. That education is enhanced with three years of experience in the marketing department of Procter and Gamble.

• *Solid understanding of marketing fundamentals, qualitative/quantitative research, marketing strategies, and ability to manage budgets.*	• *Education and experience provided me solid understanding of marketing fundamentals. I work with qualitative and quantitative research methods on a daily basis. I wrote and directed the writing of ad copy for multiple medias managing advertising budgets for up to $3 million dollars.*
• *Passion for sports.*	• *In high school, I played varsity soccer and baseball. I attended Penn State on an athletic scholarship where I played baseball for three years until I was in a car accident where I broke my arm. My pitching arm was never the same after that, but my love for sports never waned, and I still enjoy running, weight lifting, swimming, snowboarding, and flag football.*

One thing to remember about using bullets is that they will take up real estate on your one-page cover letter, particularly when using the above format. So, be mindful of what information you are trying to convey with the bulleted list. Is it important enough to sacrifice space for other information? Additionally, if you find that your cover letter seems shorter than you would like it, a bulleted list will flesh it out. While you are writing in a restricted space for a cover letter, you don't want it to be shorter than a full page.

Making Your Letter Scannable

You may be asking yourself what this even means. Making your letter scannable simply means making it machine-readable. Many companies now scan résumés into a database and then search key words for candidates who match specific requirements. To be scannable, your résumé should not contain italics, underlining, or graphics, and the font should be clear, readable, and at least 11 points.

Some companies will scan cover letters along with résumés. If you wish to make sure your cover letter can be read by these database programs, simply eliminate any formatting that would cause the program to lose words of your cover letter. That way, you can ensure that your letter is accurately uploaded into the company's database.

Additionally, the use of keyword searches is a good reason why you should know the key phrases a hiring executive in your industry will be looking for, so that you can highlight them in your cover letter and résumé.

CHAPTER 7

Phrasing – Good and Bad

As mentioned early on, your cover letter is a vehicle to display your personality to your potential employer. However, it is a compact vehicle designed to go a long distance on minimal fuel. It is a short document, no longer than one page, and the "meat" of your cover letter will be addressed in three to five paragraphs. Therefore, it is essential that the phrasing you use in those paragraphs makes an immediate positive impression.

If you are the type of person who is uncomfortable "bragging" about your accomplishments, you must overcome your natural humility when writing your cover letter. While you do not want to come off as boastful, you must portray yourself as capable of doing the job and confident in your abilities. The meek might inherit the earth, but they will not land a great job.

You are selling a great commodity with your cover letter and résumé: yourself. If you do not believe in that commodity, your audience will not want to purchase it. Your cover letter is your commercial. Television commercials are usually 30-second spots. In 30 seconds, the advertiser has to catch your attention, make you remember their product, and make you want to buy it.

You don't have much longer than that with your cover letter.

Think of something you love — something you are positively passionate about. Think of something that you love to convince your friends to try. Think of a cause you believe in — a cause you want to convince your friends and family to support. You should talk about yourself with the same gusto and enthusiasm as you do that product or cause. The following guidelines will aid you in your quest to sell yourself with fire and passion in your cover letter:

Writing Guidelines

Write in active voice.

In sentences written in active voice, the subject of the sentence performs the action expressed in the verb used.

> *The cat scratched the little girl.*

> *Jane will present papers at the conference.*

In sentences written in passive voice, the subject of the sentence receives the action being expressed by the verb.

> *The little girl was scratched by the cat.*

> *Papers will be presented by Jane at the conference.*

Active voice is more dynamic than passive voice and is generally the preferred style for all writing assignments. In a cover letter, it conveys the message to your reader that you are the one performing, rather than having things done to you. Additionally, it is a tighter form of writing — using fewer words to say the same thing.

Write in the simple tense.

Along with writing in active voice, you need to be aware of what tense you are using when you write. You are probably conjuring up bad memories of diagramming sentences as you read this, thinking that you barely survived high school grammar, so there is no way you are going to remember all that information now.

The good news is that my advice is not that complicated. For cover letter writing, you should use the simple tense whenever possible. This will allow you to keep your word count down and keep your sentences dynamic.

Consider the differences between the following examples:

I have a great passion for teaching.

I am a passionate instructor.

I have attached my résumé for your review.

I attached my résumé for your review.

Ten years of nursing experience in the emergency room has given me diverse training.

With ten years of emergency room nursing experience, I am diversely trained.

It is vitally important that you use every opportunity to shorten your message in a cover letter without losing impact. Writing in the simple tense and eliminating words like "have" when appropriate is an excellent way to achieve that goal.

Use assertive language.

Avoid using phrases like "I believe" or "I think" in your cover letter. You don't want to give the impression of "I think I can" to your reader. State firmly what you can do for them.

In doing this, it is important to use action words in your cover letter. Hiring directors may do nothing but skim your cover letter looking for certain phrases or buzz words showing you have the skills they need. It is important that you do research on the specific skill sets of your industry (the required skills of an advertised position is a good place to start) and use action words to show that you possess those skills.

The following page lists several action words you might be able to use in your writing. This is not a complete list, but it should inspire you to think about the things you have done in your career.

Action words:

Acted	Adapted	Addressed	Administered
Advanced	Advertised	Advised	Allocated
Analyzed	Appraised	Approved	Appointed
Arranged	Articulated	Assembled	Assigned
Audited	Authored	Automated	Balanced
Budgeted	Built	Calculated	Catalogued
Chaired	Coded	Collaborated	Collected
Communicated	Compiled	Completed	Composed

Computed	Conceptualized	Conducted	Consolidated
Contracted	Contributed	Controlled	Converted
Coordinated	Counseled	Created	Critiqued
Customized	Cut	Debugged	Decreased
Delegated	Demonstrated	Designed	Developed
Diagnosed	Directed	Dispatched	Distinguished
Diversified	Drafted	Edited	Educated
Eliminated	Enabled	Encouraged	Enforced
Engineered	Enhanced	Established	Evaluated
Examined	Executed	Expanded	Expedited
Extracted	Facilitated	Fashioned	Forecasted
Formulated	Fortified	Founded	Furthered
Generated	Guided	Headed	Hired
Identified	Illustrated	Implemented	Improved
Increased	Informed	Initiated	Innovated
Inspected	Installed	Instituted	Instructed
Integrated	Interviewed	Introduced	Invented
Launched	Led	Managed	Marketed
Mediated	Moderated	Monitored	Motivated
Negotiated	Operated	Organized	Originated
Overhauled	Performed	Planned	Prepared
Presented	Prioritized	Processed	Produced
Programmed	Projected	Promoted	Provided
Publicized	Published	Purchased	Reconciled
Recorded	Recruited	Reduced	Regulated
Remodeled	Repaired	Reported	Researched
Restored	Restructured	Retrieved	Revitalized
Saved	Screened	Solidified	Solved
Specified	Spoke	Standardized	Stimulated
Streamlined	Strengthened	Summarized	Supervised
Systemized	Tested	Trained	Trimmed
Upgraded	Wrote		

Make your message tight.

Even if you obey the cardinal rule of limiting yourself to a one-page cover letter, it is still possible to ramble in the three to five paragraphs allotted. The goal of your cover letter is to say as much as you can in as few words as possible. In the interest of doing that, consider the following recommendations:

Eliminate unnecessary words.

Adjectives and adverbs serve a very important role in day-to-day language and writing. They are wonderful ways to project personality and flare into your work. For that purpose, they have a place in your cover letter. However, you must be selective in how you use them.

For example, what is the significant difference in the following two sentences?

> *I greatly enjoyed our telephone conversation regarding the freelance technical writing position you are looking to fill.*

> *I enjoyed our telephone conversation regarding the freelance technical writing position you are looking to fill.*

Words like greatly, really, and very are unnecessary in cover letter writing. When I sat down to interview Danny Huffman for this book, this was one of the first things he pointed out to me. What portrays greater excitement?

> *I'm excited, I'm really excited, or I'm really, really excited.*

If the meaning of your words would not be altered by eliminating an adjective or adverb, it may be best to cut it. However, if the use of an adjective or adverb adds to the message you are trying to convey, keep it in.

Example:

> My **diverse** educational background afforded me both classroom knowledge and practical hands-on experience.

The use of the word "diverse" in this sentence may indicate the person has attended several institutions or training programs, and they want the reader to get the message that while they are new to the industry, their education is not limited.

Eliminate run-on sentences.

Your letter will be more effective when it is written with short, punchy sentences. Run-on sentences should be completely eliminated. Not only are they space killers, but if you are talking too much about one specific point, you will miss the opportunity to address others for lack of space. A good target for your sentence length is between 15 and 25 words. If it is longer than that, find a way to break it up.

Consider the following before-and-after example of how to take a run-on sentence and tighten it into a short statement that makes an impact.

Run-on:

> When I worked as the office manager for Taylor and Jackson Law Firm I performed standard office duties, maintaining the phone

lines, scheduling appointments, answering e-mails, relaying information between partners and paralegals, and I also ran errands to the court house dropping off important documents, and I spent the rest of my time researching information for the attorneys.

Statement with an impact:

As office manager at Taylor and Jackson Law Firm, I relayed information between partners and paralegals, handled confidential documents, researched court decisions, and managed a busy office of 50 plus employees.

Eliminate tacit information.

Tacit information is that which is implied or already known. A couple of examples of this were listed in the contact information section. Other examples include:

*I enjoyed our conversation about the business to business sales position you have available **with your company**.*

The position available is naturally with the hiring director's company. This is not necessarily a glaring mistake, but it is phrasing that can be edited out.

*I appreciate your consideration, and I look forward to meeting with you **in person**.*

In this case, the "in person" is implied and can be left out. Additionally, since you would not turn down a telephone or web-cam interview, it might be best not to pigeonhole yourself.

*I am **interested in working for your company**.*

The process of submitting your cover letter and résumé tells the hiring authority that you are interested in working for their company. You do not need to state it explicitly.

Never, ever be redundant:

You have a very limited amount of space to convey your message to your reader — don't waste it. Consider the following example:

> I enjoyed our **telephone conversation** regarding the freelance writing position you have available. I am interested in learning more about the unique training your company provides. Per **our conversation**, I attached my résumé for your consideration.

There is no need to point out twice that you had a telephone conversation with your reader. Choose a different word the second time around like "per your suggestion" or "per your request."

Focus on the employer — not you.

When we form relationships, we typically look for a two-way street with back-and-forth communication. Most of us don't enjoy conversations with people who are focused entirely on themselves. Your cover letter is a unique means of initial conversation. You are writing about yourself to someone who should have your entire focus. You must avoid talking about what the company can do for you, and instead, focus entirely on what you can do for them.

What can you do for me?

That is the question the hiring director wants answered as he or she skims your cover letter. What can you bring to the company? How can you make it more money? How can you increase productivity? How can you improve the system?

The answer to that question should be stated clearly in your cover letter.

Naturally, the answer will vary greatly depending on your years of experience and skill. Fortunately, how quickly the company expects to see those results will also vary, depending on the level of the position being filled.

For example, a hiring authority naturally expects that applicants to an entry-level position may need some training. However, you should not talk about how excited you are to receive that training in your cover letter like the example in the above section did with this line:

> *I am interested in learning more about the unique training your company provides.*

Instead, you should discuss what you will do with that training like the following example does:

> *After completing your specialized sales course, it will be my goal to generate 10-15 new leads per week, closing 50 percent of open cases.*

For a company looking to fill a mid-level or high-end executive position, they will want to see what results you can produce for them right now. The best way to demonstrate this is to talk about past experience, using it as an indicator of future performance.

Example:

> *Within a year of starting at my current position, I increased sales and revenue by 15 percent. After reviewing your business portfolio and your current customer base, I am confident I will bring even better results to your company.*

Overuse of the word I:

There is some debate about whether or not you should write your cover letter in the first person. Since your cover letter is an opportunity for you to convey your personality to your potential employer, I highly recommend that you stick with the first person. It is difficult to impress upon a hiring authority who you are when referring to yourself in the third person.

However, it is best to avoid an abundant use of the word "I". A cover letter should focus on the company for which you wish to work. Therefore, the abundance of the word could distract from that focus: what you can do for them.

Consider the following example, written with an "I" focus:

> *Dear Mr. Smith:*
>
> *I am interested in the position of Business to Business Representative you advertised on JobWebsite.com. I believe that I can perform this job very well and I have included **my** résumé, which highlights **my** skills and qualifications, for your review.*

Note how many times that paragraph not only uses the word I, but also references back to the writer. You want to focus the attention of the letter on your potential employer.

Written with an "employer" focus:

Dear Mr. Smith:

Your *recent advertisement on www.website.com for a Business to Business Sales Representative appears to be an excellent match for my skills and qualifications. With over eight years of experience in sales generation and customer service, which is detailed in the attached résumé, I meet* **your** *requirements in the following ways:*

It is also best, whenever possible, not to start paragraphs and sentences with I. Listing skills and accomplishments with bullets can help keep the use of "I" to a minimum, but you can list skills and accomplishments in paragraph format without overdoing it as well. Consider the following two examples and how they contrast:

I expedited customer orders at Playground Toys Central, Inc., where I also resolved billing discrepancies and tracked shipments. I made our clients aware of new products that were becoming available in upcoming months, and I made them aware of special offers that might benefit them. I believe these skills match the requirements listed in your job opening.

Among my duties at Playground Toys Central, Inc., I was responsible for all shipping concerns, including expediting orders, resolving billing discrepancies and tracking shipments. Additionally, I appraised clients of special offers and new product releases that might benefit them. These functions directly relate to the listed duties included in your posting.

Once again, the second paragraph uses the word "I," but not as much as the first. It focuses once again on the hiring authority in the final sentence, rather than the opinion of the applicant.

Write clean.

Avoid messiness:

In those instances where you will mail your cover letter and résumé, they need to be pristine documents.

In my junior year of high school, my American Literature instructor insisted that we submit rough drafts of every assignment we turned in. It did not matter if corrections were made on our computers. We were required to print a copy and make it look like we hand-edited it. He once told us to give it to our younger siblings and let them get peanut butter and jelly stains on it if we had to — he wanted a rough draft.

Your readers will not. A hiring director does not want to see a cover letter or résumé that has been crumpled up, dog-eared, has stains on it, or hand-written corrections.

Don't Do This!

Perhaps the best way to show you what to avoid is to give you a sample of a badly written cover letter. Consider how the following cover letter attempts to win the award "Worst Cover Letter Ever Written," and follow the point-by-point break-down of what the writer did wrong:

Robert S. Smith
8739 Apple Blossom Blvd.
Orlando, FL 34847 **(1)**

To whom it may concern, **(2)**

I saw your ad for a sales manager in the paper and I thought I would try my luck and send some thing in **(5)**. *I definitely think I am the guy you are looking for. I have all the skillz* **(3)** *you have listed there plus I am very easy to work with. You can call my old boss, Mr. Sheridan, at 555-555-5555 and ask him.*

I went through the list of stuff that you wanted in an employee and I have alot **(4)** *of those qualifications. You said you wanted 5 years of sales experience. I don't have that much, but I think I have at least two years* **(6)**. *But I feel I bring more to the table than just sales. I belong to an internet "group" that specializes in getting free software. I can certainly help you save money by providing you with all the software that you need. Additionally, I have a degree in psychology. I think this helps me sell products better be-cause I have a better understanding of what makes people "tick." I can read people like a book, and I can match my sales pitch so that they will hear what they want to hear. Lol* **(3)**, *they may not always like what they get, but it's usually too late* **(7)**. *We'll have the sale by then. I am a great coworker as well. I'm usually the one that organizes all the company happy hours, but I make sure everyone that goes gets home safely. No drinking and driving on my watch! I believe this makes me very valuable in boosting morale in any company. You would be very lucky to have me around your water cooler! I can also be very discrete when necessary. I know there are alot* **(4)** *of things that go on in many companies that many people, like the government, or the stockholders, dont* **(4)** *necessarily want to know about. I know when and how to keep my mouth shut* **(8)**!

Anyway, I hope I have given you some good reasons to look over my résumé and give me an interview. I think you would be stupid **(9)** *to pass up on an employee such as myself. I work hard, I play* *harder, and overall your company would be so much better if I were a part of it. Please call me as soon as you can so I can put you on my calendar* **(4)**.

Regards,

Steve Smith **(10)**

1. The Author has submitted incomplete contact information. You are far more likely to be contacted via telephone or e-mail than through your physical address.

2. While there are times when you will not know the person you are addressing your letter to, make sure you have done everything in your power to find out. When you do not know who to address your letter to, "Dear Sir/Ma'am" or "Dear Hiring Authority" reads better than "To whom it may concern."

3. Do not use slang or Internet abbreviations.

4. Use a spell and grammar checker to catch these types of typos.

5. The general tone of this letter lacks professionalism. It is lazily written and would likely be discarded with this opening sentence.

6. When addressing the requirements in an advertisement, do not state that you lack the experience required unless you can demonstrate effectively how you have acquired the necessary skills through other experience.

7. This example is extreme, but do not use inappropriate humor in your cover letters. What you might believe comes off as an "ice breaker" will likely get your résumé sent straight to the recycle bin.

8. Once again, this example is extreme, but there is something to be said for making sure what you consider an asset to a company, other people would deem an asset as well. If you aren't sure about something you are listing being perceived as a positive, ask a friend or colleague to examine your cover letter and offer advice on its contents.

9. Many experts will advise you to conclude with an aggressive statement. However, there is such a thing as being too aggressive. Comments like "you would be stupid to pass me up" or "you would come to regret missing out on the opportunity to have me as an employee" are over-the-top and should be omitted.

10. The signature of this letter is not consistent with the contact information given. Even though the middle initial of the contact information is an "S," a middle name should not be used in a signature unless the full name has been given as part of the contact information.

The comedy of that cover letter aside, it did serve to highlight several mistakes you can avoid. See the list on the following page for other common grammatical errors you can avoid.

Common Grammatical Mistakes to Avoid

They're/Their/There:

- *They're* is a contraction of the words "they are." (*They're going to the park.*)

- *Their* is a possessive pronoun indicating ownership. (*Benji is their dog.*)

- *There* is an adverb that means "in or at that place." It is used to tell where something is. (*The ball is over there.*)

It's/Its:

- *It's* is a contraction of the words "it is." (*It's a hot day today!*)

- *Its* is a possessive pronoun indicating ownership. (*Put the chair over in its place.*)

Two/Too/To:

- *Two* refers to the number.

- *Too* means "in addition to" or "also." (*She has four cats and a dog too.*) It can also mean more than what should be, very, or extremely. (*That color is too bright. I am too excited!*)

- *To* serves as a preposition or an adverb.

You're/Your:

- *You're* is a contraction of the words "you are." (*You're going to the store after work?*)

- *Your* is a possessive pronoun indicating ownership. (*Your company. Your car.*)

Affect/Effect:

- *Affect* is a verb. (*Your ability to communicate clearly will affect the outcome of the meeting.*)

- *Effect* is a noun. Think cause and effect. (*The cause was the storm; the effect was the fallen building.*)

Loose/Lose:

- *Loose* is the opposite of tight.

- *Lose* means you have had something taken away from you, or you have failed to win.

Alot:

- This is incorrect. It is always *a lot*.

Who's/Whose:

- *Who's* is a contraction of the words "who is." (*Who's going to see the movie?*)

- *Whose* indicates possession. (*Whose dog is that? Brandy, whose mother is sick, will not be here today.*)

CHAPTER 8

Medium Matters

The introduction to this book emphasized how the electronic age has changed the job-hunting process and the importance of cover letters. It is now very likely that the vast majority of résumés and cover letters that you will submit over the course of your career will be done via e-mail. "Hitting the pavement" has been replaced with "surfing the net." The information superhighway is the road you will need to navigate on your journey to a new job.

However, it is still possible that at times you will submit cover letters and résumés via fax or by mail. Some institutions still want the ability to file a physical copy of your application for their records. Sometimes the HR director simply likes to read things on paper instead of a screen. Regardless of how your cover letter and résumé are transmitted, yours will be one of hundreds — if not thousands — of entries. Therefore, this chapter will provide you with recommendations on how to ensure that your cover letters and résumé gets noticed and read through each medium — starting with electronic cover letters, then those submitted through facsimile, and finally, those submitted by mail.

Electronic Cover Letters

It is vitally important to understand the difference in delivery methods of an electronic cover letter and résumé verses that of a faxed or mailed one. When your cover letter and résumé are submitted via facsimile or through the mail, there is a paper document sitting in front of your target audience. You can rely somewhat on that person being environmentally conscious enough not to waste that paper without at least perusing your entry a little. There is no such deterrent to hitting the delete button for your e-mail.

Therefore, listed below are a few guidelines to follow in order to prevent your entire e-mail from landing in the "trash" folder:

Create a clear subject line.

How many times have you sent an e-mail to a friend without a subject line entry? Your friend knows your name and e-mail address and they are likely to open it without needing an announcement indicating what's enclosed. If you are feeling particularly verbose, you might type in a subject line that reads: "from Steve," "too funny," or "read this."

These sorts of generic subject lines will not work when submitting your job packet electronically. Think of your subject line as the headline to a newspaper or magazine article. It tells your reader whether this is an e-mail they want to open and read. But do not try to be cute or amusing. Make sure your subject line is clear, attention grabbing, and professional all at the same time.

Often, when you are responding to an advertisement that directs you to submit your cover letter and résumé to a specific e-mail address, they will tell you to type something specific in the subject line. If that is the case, do it.

Examples:

> To all applicants: Please place this job ID: 46526 in your subject line as well as the title of the position you are applying for.

> When applying for this position, mention job id 010109-10 in your subject line.

> Please send cover letter and résumé to hireme@email.com and note the position you are applying for in the subject line.

If not, you must be very clear what the contents of your e-mail are in your subject line. You do not want your reader to consider your e-mail nothing more than "spam" or "junk mail." This is particularly important when sending a cold-call letter or an e-mail to a headhunter. These people are less likely to be looking for your e-mail than a human resources director compiling applications for an advertised position. Only an eye-catching, clear subject line is going to save your e-mail from the "trash" folder.

Consider the following sample subject lines:

Subject lines to an advertisement –

> Résumé and writing samples for feature reporter opening.

> Résumé highlighting 15 years of sales experience.

Subject lines to a headhunting firm –

Résumé from experienced system administrator.

Résumé from highly productive office manager.

Subject lines for an unsolicited résumé –

Jane Smith suggested I send you my résumé.

Award-winning salesperson submitting résumé for your consideration.

Deliver your message.

Once you have composed a subject line that will ensure your e-mail is opened, you must decide how you will attach your cover letter. You have two options: type your cover letter directly into your e-mail or include it as an attachment.

If you choose to attach your cover letter, you should still include a brief note in your e-mail introducing yourself, stating why you are writing, and stating what attachments came with the e-mail. People are not necessarily going to open e-mailed attachments without knowing who sent them. This is one of the reasons why it may be best to send paper cover letters and résumés when sending "broadcast" letters since your audience will neither know you nor will they have advertised for applications.

A short introductory note may look something like this:

Dear Mr. Anderson,

Thank you for your kind consideration in reading this e-mail. I have attached my résumé and a cover letter in regard to your job posting for a junior sales representative. I hope you find my ex-

perience and skills compatible to your team, and I look forward to hearing from you after you have reviewed my attachments.

Sincerely,

Dana Morgan

If, on the other hand, you choose to type your cover letter directly into your e-mail, some experts recommend cutting out the "letter" look and opting for something more like the following sample:

Dear Mr. Hart,

As a recent MBA graduate from Florida State University with over ten years of solid sales experience, I am an ideal candidate for the regional sales manager position at Family Vacation Club.

Having exceeded quotas or broken sales records in all my previous positions, I will make an immediate positive impact on your company training others to duplicate my success.

As one of the leading sales representatives for Florida Vacation Club, I was part of the team that redesigned how club memberships were sold, increasing our customer satisfaction rate by 25 percent. My team's revenue was double the average for the entire operation, and I served as a professional developer designing sales material and training new sales representatives.

Please review my attached résumé and I will contact you next week to arrange an interview. Should you have any questions before that time, please feel free to call me at 904-555-2341 or e-mail me. Thank you for your time and consideration.

Respectfully,

Keri Smith

This format has the benefit of being short enough that the person who opens the e-mail will be able to read it without having to scroll down, which is ideal. It however does not present your reader with as much detail as an average cover letter, but if written well enough, it may suffice. The most important thing this cover letter achieves is that it presents the reader with immediate information without requiring them to open an attachment. For some people, that may be necessary to grab their attention and gain you consideration.

Be brief and to the point.

Throughout this book, the brevity of a cover letter has been emphasized. This rule intensifies in electronic cover letters. Whether you are typing your cover letter directly into the body of the e-mail or simply including a brief introductory note, as mentioned in the previous section, it is ideal that the length of the cover letter be limited to that which a person can see on their screen without having to scroll up and down. The less you make your reader work, the more likely they are to read your information in its entirety.

Follow up.

The advantage of an electronically submitted cover letter and résumé is that you may hear from a hiring authority within days of submission, rather than weeks if you had submitted your cover letter and résumé by mail. However, it is very easy for your e-mail to get lost in a sea of e-mails that the hiring director receives every day. Therefore, it is important that you follow up with an in-person form of communication whenever possible. A courtesy call is often the best way to give the HR personnel a slight "nudge" in opening and looking over your documents.

Include your résumé.

This particular point may seem obvious, but you do not want to send your e-mail out without your résumé included in some fashion. There might be specific instructions when responding to an advertisement telling you how to submit your résumé. It might inform you to save your résumé as a .txt document or to cut and paste it into the body of your e-mail. However, when those specific instructions are not present, you have several options to choose from:

- Paste it into the body of the e-mail. This is the easiest method, but definitely not recommended. The formatting of your résumé will likely be lost using this method and you will, in effect, be hitting your reader with a wall of text. Different e-mail systems handle the format of incoming mail in their own way. Some may leave your résumé and cover letter as is, but many will reformat it in some fashion, often throwing away all the work you've done in making your résumé look just right. In addition to not looking the way you had intended your résumé to look, your résumé will probably look very sloppy, very disorganized, and very much something that your intended audience does not want to read.

- Send your résumé as an attachment, saved as a word processing file. Microsoft Word is the industry standard for word processing files, but if you are not using that program, you still might be able to save your document as a Word-compatible file. Check your "Save as" options in your computer. Additionally, if you are using Microsoft Word 2007, you have the option to "Save as" a Word 97-2003 document. This is highly recommended. If your target audience is still using an older version of Word, they will not be able to open a Word 2007 saved document. The important thing to note is that an older document will be saved as résumé.doc compared to résumé.docx, which is the Word 2007 document.

- Attach your résumé in another format — PDF or RTF.

  PDF stands for portable document format. You can create one using a program called Adobe Acrobat. Some programs can save documents in PDF format as well. An advantage of using this format is that all formatting is retained, but the recipient does not need to have Microsoft Word or any other specific piece of software to open and read your document. The downside is that your résumé will be saved as a graphic and not a text document, and therefore, cannot easily be entered into a résumé tracking system that many companies use. Additionally, the receiver will need a program like Adobe Acrobat Reader that will open the document.

RTF stands for rich text format. It can be advantageous to save your document as RTF if you know your reader will not be able to open your document in a Word program. RTF formatting is very widely recognized by many word processing programs. However, this type of formatting strips the document down to the bare bones and loses the formatting you put into it. Therefore, it is only recommended to attach your résumé in this form if you are specifically instructed to do so.

- Include your résumé as part of a web portfolio and reference the URL in the body of your e-mail. If you choose this option, it is still best to attach a text résumé as well. This option might be particularly useful for someone who needs to highlight a lot of visual achievements, like a photographer or interior designer. If you use this option, be sure to devote the entire site to your professional portfolio. Do not let a family Web site play double duty to your job hunt.

Avoid Internet slang.

The Internet revolutionized communication. With the introduction of e-mail, blogging, texting, and instant messaging, we can multi-task like never before. You can be on a phone call with a customer, e-mailing your mother, instant messaging a friend in Chicago, and texting your boyfriend about dinner plans. With this new world of communication came a language all its own — a new form of slang, to be precise. While most of us do not use this slang in verbal communication (though some teenagers may be caught saying "OMG" instead of "Oh my God"), it is infesting written communications in force. As a college professor, I found Internet abbreviations such as **u** instead of **you** regularly in papers I graded. An electronically submitted cover letter is not the place for lazy writing, and it is definitely not the place for **LOL, OMG, u r, u 2**, or other such slang. All of these abbreviations should be omitted from any electronic follow-up communication as well.

Spell and grammar check your e-mail.

It is very likely that your e-mail program has some sort of spell check in it. However, I would still recommend that you write your cover letter in a word program and copy and paste it into your e-mail once it is completely composed. In addition to having a spelling and grammar checker, it is possible that typing your cover letter in word format will help you avoid the mistakes mentioned above. I would recommend doing this even if you intend to attach your cover letter as a word document and are only writing a brief note in your e-mail body.

I make this recommendation because you simply see more errors in e-mail than you do in mailed letters. Beyond using a word program to avoid the common mistakes of e-mail, here are some specific errors to watch out for:

- Random capitalization: Do not capitalize a word to make a point. Do NOT use all caps for emphasis either.

- Missing capitalizations: As bad as it is to see random words improperly capitalized, it is far worse to see no capitalization at all. People might not capitalize the start of a sentence when instant messaging, but it is not a sign of effective communication to write a letter entirely in lower case.

- Use proper spacing after commas and periods. A word processing program will almost certainly point out this mistake to you, but it could easily be missed when writing directly into the body of your e-mail.

- Additionally, break up your paragraphs. Do not hit your reader with a wall of text that is visually unappealing. Insert spaces between your paragraphs to make your document easier to read and understand.

Remember, if your cover letter text is not readable because of spelling or grammatical errors, the chances of getting your résumé read, and subsequently getting called in for an interview, are significantly diminished.

Be plain.

If you choose to type your cover letter directly into the body of the e-mail you are sending, you should use the default font of your e-mail program. Although you can get fancy and include types of highlighting and dramatic formatting, you should not do this. As previously mentioned, some experts will even recommend that you abandon the traditional cover letter format, opting instead to work contact information (like your phone number) into the body of your cover letter or include it at the bottom of your e-mail underneath your typed signature.

If you decide to copy and paste a cover letter from a word processing program into your e-mail, rethink that decision. While it may be possible to do this, you need to understand that different e-mail programs and readers will chop, slice, dice, and blend your e-mail to whatever format they desire. Your résumé may look fantastic on your computer, but it may look completely strange after being processed by your recipient's e-mail system.

If you still decide to copy and paste, change the e-mail to plain text so that your e-mail will transmit as closely as possible to the message you see on your screen as you prepare it. RTF- or HTML-based e-mail will look better, but the differences in how e-mail systems translate those formats will put your cover letter and résumé at risk, and it may look like a jumbled mess on the other side of the computer screen.

No matter how you decide to transmit your e-mailed cover letter, the most important things you can do are to keep it brief, readable, and give it a meaningful subject line so that it gets opened.

Faxed Cover Letters

Submitting a faxed cover letter is somewhat simpler than submitting one sent by e-mail. This process will be very similar to mailing your cover letter in to a physical address. Here are a few simple recommendations for the faxed cover letter:

- Prepare a neat cover sheet that includes your name, a return fax number, and the number of pages that should be included in the fax.

- Position the order of the papers being faxed so that your cover letter will appear on top of your résumé and so that your résumé will appear in order after it is transmitted.

- Make sure your entire fax packet is labeled with your name so that if a page is lost, that it is clear to the person on the receiving end, and they can look for a missing page, or contact you to re-submit your package.

- Unless specifically instructed not to, follow up with a phone call shortly after sending your résumé to make sure it was received in its entirety.

Mailed Cover Letters

When sending your cover letter and résumé by mail, follow these recommendations:

- Use high-quality paper for printing in a standard size. You may use shaded paper in colors such as cream, ivory, or light gray in an effort to stand out, but avoid bold colors or patterned backgrounds.

- Submit your entire job package (e.g., cover letter, résumé, enclosures) in a document folder so the pages are not folded and it appears neat and professional when it arrives. This may cost a bit more in postage, but it looks more professional, and your recipients will appreciate the effort.

- Position your cover letter on top so that your reader will view it first.

PART THREE

SAMPLES

CHAPTER 9

Sample Cover Letters for Students and Graduates

As mentioned throughout this book, your cover letter is an extremely tailored document that may vary according to your target audience. But your cover letter is also tailored to you, and the differences between a cover letter written by a recent engineering graduate and a marketing executive with 20 years of experience are vast.

You have seen sample cover letters used to demonstrate specific points or compare and contrast certain elements of cover letter writing. In this section of the book, the sample cover letters will be used to demonstrate specific recommendations for people at different points in their careers in different industries.

This chapter will address those at the start of their career, or the start of a new career: students and recent graduates. This may apply to someone who transitioned from high school to college and is graduating at 22, ready to enter the workforce with little- to-no "real world" experience. Or, it may apply to someone who just worked their way through college holding down a full-time job at any age and brings with them significant work experience.

Naturally, someone who went back to school later in life to change careers or obtain an advanced degree will have more experience to draw on as they enter or reenter the workforce. An "adult learner" should not only draw on their academic achievement, but also on their real world experience as they present themselves as a job candidate for a hiring authority. Even if that job experience is in another career, certain skills may be relevant in your new career as well. In the last chapter of this book, advice is given for individuals looking for a career change that may apply here as well. Otherwise, continue reading for recommendations on how to handle the academic achievements you wish to highlight in your résumé and cover letter.

Academic Experience

As a student or recent graduate, the bulk of your résumé and cover letter will be spent referencing your academic career. It is likely that the majority of what you have to highlight will come from what you achieved and learned in school. That's perfectly fine. After all, that is why you were in school. You can use any or all of the following in your cover letter:

Course work and GPA:

If you don't have the best grade point average in the world and you are nervous about having to include that on your résumé, don't stress it. Huffman says that, "According to the top three career management associations, if a student has a 3.0 GPA or above, it is recommended to state it."

Otherwise, you can leave it off. You may still have to address this subject in an interview, but much like a low grade point average won't necessarily keep you out of graduate school, a low GPA won't eliminate you from job consideration if you can properly explain you reasons (working a full-time job to pay for school or family stresses) or show how you've grown since then (you partied your first two semesters and got on academic probation, but worked your tail off to bring your grades up and graduate).

The thing to remember about your GPA is that it should be used only if it benefits you to do so.

Clubs and Organizations:

Huffman says to use membership in clubs and other organizations only if it highlights positive transferable skills or is directly related to the position and/or industry. Remember, as discussed earlier in this book, simply stating you possess a skill is not enough. You must show the correlation between an activity and the skill for which you claim to be qualified.

So don't list "Served as Treasurer for the Young Republicans" or "Worked as Secretary for the Young Democrats."

Instead, try:

> *"As Treasurer for the Young Republicans, I kept balanced books for three years tracking fund-raising efforts, paying invoices, collecting dues, and reporting on expenditures to the organization"*

> *"As Secretary for the Young Democrats, I kept detailed records of all meetings, preparing minutes and posting them on our Web site, tracked membership, prepared a weekly e-newsletter, and created and maintained a posting board for member communication."*

Work Experience

Work experience is vital for anyone applying for any position. But how does someone just starting out demonstrate this valuable asset? A student or recent graduate can do so in the following ways:

Internships:

For recent graduates with no significant professional experience to speak of, internships, teaching assistant positions, co-ops, and summer jobs are all excellent things to highlight on your résumé and cover letter. "Employers know the graduating student has limited experience; as such, they look for candidates displaying leadership traits, possessing a strong work/study ethic, and diverse knowledge," says Danny Huffman of Career Services International.

Work History unrelated to career:

While listing clubs and organizations should only be done if you can show a correlation between the skills you acquired as part of them and the skills you will need in your new career, previous work history can be used even if it is just a part-time retail job at your local mall.

"Showing previous work experience displays knowledge of business and expectations," says Huffman. "Very few companies want to hire an employee who has never worked a day in a formal setting. Even flipping burgers carries weight — perhaps you trained fellow peers or handled a schedule. Dealing with clients in all types of settings carries value."

Other Questions

Many students or recent graduates might make the mistake of including too much information in their cover letter. Perhaps you are tempted to state that you will work for any amount or move anywhere. Read the following recommendations first:

The Salary Question:

Many applicants are reluctant to handle the salary questions. Recent graduates and students might think it is a good idea to mention they will work for less because the experience is such a great opportunity. Huffman says not to do it. In fact, he said to never mention salary. This is a subject best addressed in an interview.

Relocation:

Willingness to move is almost a given with applications coming from students and recent graduates. You do not need to state that you are willing to relocate, though you might want to mention a time period when you will be in town if you plan to travel to the city where you are applying for a position. This will make it easier for a hiring authority to schedule an interview with you.

Cover Letter Samples

Consider the following cover letters, for students and recent graduates which combine the above recommendations:

To further assist you, some of the following cover letters include the font names and font sizes in which they were originally written. Also, If the letter was provided by a contributor, his or her name is also included; see the "Contributors" page for more details.

Cover Letter from a recent college graduate for an editorial position:

Mr. Brown,

I'm the daughter of two chemists and sister to a lawyer and an Army sergeant, so my career choice is always a hot topic. But I've always known I wanted to be a journalist.

I kept daily diaries in spiral-bound notebooks and read Cameron Crowe and Rick Bragg instead of the Babysitters' Club. I thrive under the long hours, the stressful deadlines and yes, even the bizarre tactics we have to sometimes use to snag interviews.

For me, the juice is totally worth the squeeze.

My enthusiasm for journalism stems from my passion for music, which I inherited from my father, a music major turned chemist who now plays bass in an Atlanta jazz band. I left the city three years ago and moved to Florida for school. I already had the passion: I just needed to learn the technique.

There, I was hurtled into one of the most prestigious journalism departments. There, I got experience.

As the local news and entertainment intern at The Gainesville Sun, I covered whatever an editor threw my way. As the music intern at Creative Loafing, I covered Atlanta music news for their online department. I didn't walk away with any hard-copy clips, but I learned how to blog, link and tag: I learned the Web.

As the managing editor for That Girl!, I supervised a 15-person team to create an original magazine prototype. I researched, report-

ed and managed; I produced a four-photographer, multi-location photo shoot; I designed the Web site – www.mywebsite.com – and the business plan. I picked up what others didn't do.

As an assistant producer on the 2008 Florida FlyIns Documentary, I got my first glimpse into broadcast journalism. I logged tape and edited clips. I learned Final Cut Pro. I loved it.

Now, as the editor in chief of Orange and Blue, I manage a 29-member team to design, edit and produce a 72-page magazine. I coordinate deadlines, final edit articles and mediate discussion. I brainstorm stories, assign articles and produce photo shoots.

But being the **editorial assistant** at Atlantic Publishing Company would give me the experience I need to continue practicing my passion. Why? Because it would allow me to take my fundamental journalism skills to do what I do best: edit.

Thank you so much for considering me for the editorial assistant position at Atlantic Publishing Company. I've attached a copy of my résumé and some sample clips, and additional clips are available online at www.myclips.com.

Thank you again, and I look forward to hearing from you.

Erin Everhart
erineverhart@email.com
(404) 545-6052
www.website.com

Cover Letter from a recent college graduate for an advertised position:

KAREN THOMAS
4559 S. Tennessee Ave.
Lake, Fl 33801
KSThomasFL@email.com
(432) 555-3843

Dear Mr. Julian Webb:

*As a recent college graduate with a B.S. in Communication from the University of South Florida, I understand why you might not consider me a strong candidate for your **assistant editor** opening. But my résumé should demonstrate to you that I received more than just an education in my time at USF — I received practical, hands-on experience that makes me competitive in today's difficult job market.*

Any writer will tell you they have a passion for the written word. I want to show you more than my passion — I want to show you that I can do the job as well as my competitors who might have more professional experience than I do.

To meet that goal, let me highlight a few aspects of my attached résumé:

- *I wrote and edited for the campus newspaper. As a student reporter, I published in-depth investigative reports on the counseling that victims of date-rape were receiving at our campus. The series of articles won national honors at the college newspaper convention last year.*

- *The summer of 2008, I interned at the Chicago Times. I was one of a dozen interns selected to work in one of the busiest* newsrooms in the country. I spent 12-hour days copywriting countless stories. At the end of my internship, my supervisor, Jack Brown, said my work was incredible and he would gladly serve as a professional reference for me.

- I worked on the college's online newspaper for course credit last fall. In this course, I learned about page layout, web design, and HTML. Besides writing original content, I also wrote all headlines and photo captions for the paper. It was an invaluable experience, as it made me confident I can handle online duties in the area of Internet news.

I would enjoy meeting with you to further discuss whether I am the right fit for your office. I look forward to hearing from you in the near future to schedule an interview.

Sincerely,

Karen Thomas

Cover Letter from a recent college graduate for an editorial position:

Atlantic Publishing Company, Mr. Brown
1210 SW 23rd Place
Ocala, FL 34474

April 1, 2009

Dear Mr. Brown:

For the better part of my college career, I've been the journalism major who ignored the news. I went through the past three years of my life virtually uninformed. It was almost as if I was immune to *any form of news — papers, online and television. Instead, I found pleasure in the ability to lose myself within the pages of a magazine, catching up on the latest fashion and health trends. Journalism, as I knew it, was simply a form of entertainment.*

This summer, I changed, although not intentionally.

As an intern at WESH 2 News in Orlando, I was thrown in the middle of the news. My internship required that I was in the field two days a week for the sunrise shift, starting at 3:30 a.m. Engulfed in each day's news, I learned to work at a quick pace when covering a story. I grew accustomed to the sense of urgency that came with live shots, and the deadlines that followed for packaging a story. It was a rush of adrenaline, and before I knew it, I was addicted to television news. I had developed a need to be in the know.

When I returned to school, I applied for an internship at WCJB-TV 20, an ABC affiliate in Gainesville. I began learning all aspects of the news. I had the opportunity to report as a student correspondent, in addition to becoming an associate producer. As a one-man-band, I learned how to do it all, from generating story ideas and writing scripts to photography and editing the final package. It was hard work, but I still loved every minute of it.

I tried not to sacrifice one love for another. I continued to study print journalism, specifically magazines, at the University of Florida. During my junior year, I found myself the editor-in-chief of an original class prototype, That Girl! Everything I learned was coming together in one master class, as I led a student staff through the production of a 64-page prototype. It was the busiest semester of my life, and nothing could have prepared me for the amount of work, planning and creativity that came with being in charge of a magazine. There were many all-nighters spent in campus com-

puter labs, but after seeing the end product, I wouldn't trade that feeling of accomplishment, or the experience, for the world. It was my experience with TG! that led me back to an editorial position the following year, as Editor-in-Chief of UF's Orange & Blue magazine.

My ideas of what journalism is have changed over the years. I've been lucky enough to explore different media. While I love it all and believe I would be happy working in any field, working as Editor-in-Chief of both That Girl! and Orange & Blue has only validated my passion for being an editor and overseeing all stages of production.

I would appreciate the opportunity to continue to work in the ever-changing field of publishing at your company. Please consider me for a position at the Atlantic Publishing Company. I look forward to hearing from you. Thank you for your time.

Sincerely,

Nicole Orr

Cover Letter from a soon-to-graduate student to a Headhunting agency:

PAMALA BROWN

(847) 555-2827 – pbrown45@email.com

Current Address: Permanent Address:
111 Dorm Hall, FSU   2222 Roadside Drive
Tallahassee FL 38973   Tampa FL 32729

March 15, 2009

Howard Wright
Job Placement Associates
7892 Lime Street Suite 9B

Tampa FL 34821

Dear Mr. Wright:

I am an honors engineering student at Florida State University and will be graduating with a bachelor's of science in mechanical engineering in May of this year.

I am in search of an entry-level position as a project engineer in the central engineering department of a manufacturing company. I would enjoy being involved with engineering, installation, and start-up of manufacturing equipment, as well as general plant facilities engineering work.

Besides my academic achievement, I am a student athlete who has played on the school's tennis team for the last three years. I have a balanced perspective and maintain involvement in a wide range of diverse activities.

Last summer, I was an engineering intern with The Armor Hammer Company, where I worked in their central engineering department as an apprentice to the design engineer in support of plant capital projects. My supervisor will gladly serve as a referral, as will several of my professors.

Should one of your client companies have room in their organization for a bright, eager engineer, I would appreciate a call. Thank you for your time and consideration.

Sincerely

Pamala Brown

(This letter was written in Bookman Old Style in font size 10.5)

Sample Networking Letter for a soon-to-be graduate:

Sharon McReynolds
555 Fifth Ave.
New York, NY 10392
(938) 555-9392
SMReynolds@email.com

April 10, 2009

Ms. Janet Reading
Vice President Account Director
State Advertising
555 Jefferson Ave.
New York, NY 10502

Dear Ms. Reading:

Geoffrey Daniels of Last Stop Advertising suggested that I write to you. He said you began your careers together years ago writing ad copy at the New York Times. As you know, Mr. Daniels frequently guest lectures at State University. I meet him in my capacity as president of the Student Business Association. We have kept in touch ever since. After a recent conversation regarding my pursuits after graduation, he sent me your name and contact information and suggested that you might be able to assist me in my future endeavors.

With a double major in advertising and public relations, I had an exciting internship last summer for Congressman Bill Young where I gained hands on experience in market research and advertisement design. I was momentarily tempted to go into political work, but decided that I would prefer the corporate world.

I have attached my résumé for your review. Mr. Daniels made it clear that he knows of no openings in your firm at this time, but he said you would be an ideal contact for networking and assisting me in presenting myself well to potential employers. I will call you next week to see if you are available for such a meeting. Thank you very much.

Sincerely,

Sharon McReynolds

Enclosure: Résumé

Sample Cover Letter for a Recent Graduate for an Advertised Position:

DEBRA SWALTZ
3928 West Vine Blvd.
City, State 39282
(283) 555-2920
dwaltz@email.com

January 23, 2009

Janice Linville
North Eastern Press
jlinville@email.com

Dear Ms. Linville:

I am submitting my résumé in response to your advertised listing for an administrative assistant in the City Daily. Having recently graduated from City College with a B.S. in business administration, I meet your listed qualifications in the following ways:

- As secretary of the City College's Student Government, I recorded and posted minutes for all meetings; transmitted communication between students, their government, and faculty sponsors; and prepared and sent a weekly e-newsletter demonstrating my ability to communicate information in an accurate, timely, and interesting way.

- Strong data entry skills learned working part-time as a research surveyor for the college's Government and Public Policy Department, where I interviewed respondents at a 75 percent closure rating.

- Strong office skills, including the ability to type 60 correct words per minute and proficiency in all Microsoft Office software, including Word, Excel, PowerPoint, and Access as evident by two related computer courses.

I would enjoy meeting with you to discuss how I can meet your needs in greater detail. I will contact you next week to schedule an interview at your convenience. Thank you for your time and consideration. I look forward to meeting you soon.

Sincerely,

Debra Swaltz

Sample Online Cover Letter for a recent Graduate:

JANET ROSENBERG
555 Belle Ave.
Davenport, IA 52807
(563) 555-8858

Dear Hiring Authority:

As a recent master's graduate looking for an opportunity to bring my education and experience to a well known, established, internationally oriented organization, I am submitting my résumé for your consideration.

I can provide the excellent quality, highly responsive service your company requires. As a recent graduate with a master's in Islamic and Middle Eastern studies, I have a background perfectly suited for a company with a global market. Having held a secret security clearance, I foresee no problems obtaining a further security clearance. Research and analysis are strong suits of mine, and I am fluent with many different types of computer programs. Having studied various languages, including four and a half years of French, seven years of Modern Hebrew, and three years of Modern Standard Arabic, I believe you will find my language skills useful to you in the international market.

As an extremely energetic, fast learner with outstanding communication skills who enjoys a challenge, I bring a tremendous amount of zeal to every job.

I look forward to speaking with you regarding my qualifications. Please know that I am willing to pay my own relocation fees. Thank you very much for your time and consideration.

Sincerely,

Janet Rosenberg

(This cover letter was prepared by contributor Shira Karp)

Applying for Internships

If you are an upper-level student with another semester or two of course work, a soon-to-be graduate or recent graduate, or a graduate student pursuing a post-bachelorette degree — internships can be an extremely sought-after position as they offer the chance to "learn the trade" while still continuing your course work, or helping a graduate get their feet wet in their chosen profession.

Because internships can be so useful when applying for entry-level positions down the road, more students and recent graduates are seeking them out as a means to get their foot into their respective industries. Some internships are advertised, but many will come through networking. I highly recommend getting to know your professors. They are not just scary people who lecture you at the front of a crowded classroom and determine your fate by red ink marks — they are professionals who have contacts in the industry. They are a great place to start the networking that will benefit you throughout your career, and you may find yourself returning to them later.

Many internships are highly sought after, and you will have to compete for them with a résumé and cover letter, much like you would for an entry-level position. The first thing that should be noted about internships is that some will be paid while many will be unpaid. Many times, you can receive college credit for internships and as such, you might be qualified for financial aid while you work one. This is particularly important if an internship is unpaid. Make sure you consult an academic advisor or department counselor on this subject.

Cover letters for internships may be as varied as cover letters for job hunting. You may be responding to an advertised internship (**solicited response**), making a contact with someone that a professor or parent suggested (**networking/referral**), or simply contacting someone at a company where you would love to someday be employed (**broadcasting**).

Between the advice you received throughout the book and the specific recommendations for students, you should be well-prepared to write a cover letter for an internship. However, there are a few differences you might want to consider:

- **DO** mention relevant coursework.

- **DO** mention honors and other achievements.

- **DO** mention hobbies or leisure activities that may relate to the internship.

Sample Cover Letters for Internships

With this in mind, consider the cover letter samples on the following pages for internships:

Sample Cover Letter for an Internship:

TRACIE GOLDMAN

PO BOX 321 – State University – Capitol, State 28291

(354) 555-9282 – tgoldman@email.com

May 1, 2009

Jack Brown
ABC Labs
5555 33rd Street, Suite #1
Capitol, State 29382

Dear Mr. Brown:

I am writing in reference to the Lab Tech Internship position listed recently on the State University Job Fair Web site. This position appeals to me because of my strong interest in working in a pharmaceutical laboratory in addition to using the knowledge I've gained through my science classes in college.

I am in my junior year at State University, with a major in Chemistry and a minor in Biology.

My strengths include:

- *Strong work ethic, demonstrated by my 3.85 GPA.*

- *The ability to work independently, as required by my laboratory projects.*

- *Accuracy, demonstrated through papers and reports with top marks.*

- *The ability to multi-task, shown by my part-time job as an after-school tutor, my volunteer work with Habitat for Humanity, and my involvement in the intramural coed rowing team.*

These skills, combined with the education I have received in my chemistry and biology courses, make me an ideal candidate for this internship position.

Enclosed, please find a current copy of my résumé and letters of recommendation. Thank you for considering me for this position. I look forward to hearing from you soon.

Sincerely,

Tracie Goldman

Sample Cover Letter for an Internship:

PATRISHA "TRISH" RICHARDSON
222 West 2nd Street,
Gainesville, FL 32608,
(123)-555 7890.

May 1, 2009.

Mr. John Smith,
USA Theme Parks
555, Park Avenue South,
New York, NY 12345.

Dear Mr. Smith:

My previous work experience, combined with my status as a marketing student at the University of Florida, makes me an ideal candidate for a summer internship with Theme Park Orlando.

My five years of retail sales experience and my education make me a good candidate, but what makes me stand out is the two summers I spent working at Theme Park Orlando between my junior and senior year and after graduation. I have first-hand knowledge of the park and its customers.

Additionally, having done some part-time modeling, I can tell you honestly that my most attractive feature is my smile. It would be my pleasure to turn that smile on for your customers at Theme Park Orlando.

I have attached my résumé so you can review my qualifications in greater detail. I will contact you within a week to arrange a meeting. Thank you for your time and consideration.

Sincerely,

Trish Richardson

(This cover letter was written in Times New Roman at font size 12).

CHAPTER 10

Samples by Industry

As a professional résumé writer, one of the things Danny Huff-man notices most about résumés posted online is that they are typically outdated. Internet templates are not individually tai-lored enough, he says. A résumé should be tailored for industry expectations, skills, and job expectations. Without that triangula-tion effect, he argues that an applicant is at a significant disad-vantage.

Much like a résumé for an electrical engineer has to differ from that of a pediatric nurse, the cover letters for these industries will differ as well. The basic structure established throughout this book will be the same, but the emphasis and flow of these letters will be different.

The most important thing that will differ from industry to in-dustry is the keywords that employers are looking to identify. I touched on keywords under the style section, when I explained how to make a cover letter "scannable." As a reminder, keywords and phrases are ones that employers are looking for in the weed-ing out process of selecting job candidates.

A hiring executive does this by sight, or they have a computer program to do it for them. The practice of "qualifying" and "disqualifying" candidates based on the absence or presence of specific words and phrases is becoming increasingly common.

This section of the book will include three things:

1. Recommendations for content to include in your industry-specific cover letter.

2. A list of keywords and phrases researched through advertisements and the Internet that may be useful for each industry.

3. Sample cover letters to show the reader how to bring the first two elements together.

Please note that the keywords and phrases in some sections are extremely lengthy. You will not have room in your cover letter to make use of all of them. Those lists are there to simply provide you with inspiration. It might be easier to pick up on the important aspects of your résumé or a job listing if you review the keywords and phrases listed under your industry. As always, tailor these recommendations to your skills and experience.

The samples provided in this section may represent any of the four types of cover letters examined in this book.

To further assist you, some of the following cover letters include the font names and font sizes in which they were originally written. Also, If the letter was provided by a contributor, his or her name is also included; see the "Contributors" page for more details.

Accounting, Banking, and Financial Careers

Be quantitative: Statistics, percentages, and numbers are the things that accounting, banking, and financial professionals work with every day; so naturally, it makes sense to use them in your cover letter. In particular, use them to highlight your skills and achievements.

Rather than say:

> *I was responsible for establishing the company's automated payment system that saved money and increased efficiency.*

Try:

> *I was responsible for establishing the company's automated payment system that saved an estimated $20,000 a year and increased efficiency by ten percent.*

Of course, you should not make these figures up. So, if you don't know the percentages or numbers, either find them out or leave them out.

Showcase your technical skills: In today's electronic information age, the software programs you know how to use can be as important as any other skill you have mastered in your career. This is valuable information to your potential employer.

Demonstrate specialties and diversity: Show off the diverse skills you possess and any special training that relates specifically to the position for which you are applying. This type of training is important to your potential employer because it is training they do not have to pay for down the line.

Consider the list of keywords and phrases on the following page:

Keywords and phrases for **Accounting, Banking and Financial Professionals:**

Accounts payable and receivable	Asset-based lending and Asset management
Auditing	Budget Control and Administration
Cash Management	Consumer/Commercial banking and lending
Corporate Treasury	Cost Accounting
Cost/Benefit Analysis	Credit and Collections
Debt Financing	Depository services
Employee Stock Ownership Plan (ESOP)	Equity financing
Financial Analysis and reporting	Foreign Exchange
Global banking	Internal Accounting controls
Investment Analysis and management	Lending and Loan Administration
Letters of credit	Loan administration
Margin improvement	Mergers and Acquisitions
Operating budgets	Partnership accounting
Portfolio management	Profit and Loss analysis
Project accounting	Regulatory Affairs
Retail banking and lending	Return on investment (ROI)
Risk management	Secondary markets
Secured and unsecured lending	Trust services

Sample "Broadcast" Cover Letter for an Investment Banker:

JIM BISHOP, MA, CFP

April 8, 2009

Ms. Rachael Linville
President
Business Inc.
111 Main St.
Atlanta, GA 48228

Dear Ms. Linville:

Development of human capital has a direct impact on your bottom line. A solid recruiting and training program can sharply increase that impact. Spending the last several years mastering practical psychology — coupled with over 15 years of senior financial management — I create value-added methodology to enhance existing training, and have the ability to create programs from scratch.

My success as a leading investment manager convinced me to pursue the next level — discovering better ways to approach turnover reduction and candidate training. Please consider my unique qualifications:

- *Contributed significant advances to varied industries with regard to strategic planning, training, leadership development, sales guidance, and recruitment.*

- *Led financial planning performance growing annual sales from $300 million to $750 million in less than two years.*

- *Designed a revolutionary new investment product that became an industry standard. Raised assets under management to over $500 million.*

- *Published two financial books and a financial column for The Dallas/Ft. Worth Times.*

In a permanent position, I can develop a complete program encompassing hiring and development of financial representatives, or I can join your current management, recruitment, or training team to further your goals. My résumé is attached and I look forward to your response.

Sincerely,

Jim Bishop, MA, CFP

Enclosure

Sample Cover Letter for an advertised Accounting position:

Susan Baker

55 Driveway Drive - Middleton TX 45372

Home: (555) 555-5556 Cell: (555) 555-5555 — sbarker@email.com

May 1, 2009

Mr. Gary Robinson
Hiring Manager
Brown Shoe Company
111 Shoe Street. Suite 11
Middleton TX 45938

RE: Job posting for Accountant (#2728)

Dear Mr. Robinson:

*Your listing on www.website.com said you were in need of an **Accountant** with a proven history of accuracy, accountability, and integrity. With over ten years of experience in the corporate world and five years in business for myself, I offer all of that and more as my clients will attest.*

Highlight of my professional career include:

• *Experience in accounts receivable, billing, credit/collection, accounts payable, and accounting/financial reporting for companies as small as ten employees to large corporations.*

• *Being on the forefront of computer programming to automate offices and make accounting procedures go smoother.*

• *Experience in customer relations as a personal accountant and as a corporate accountant assisting in negotiating mergers and acquisitions.*

After you have the opportunity to review my résumé, I would like to meet with you to discuss how I can effectively contribute to Brown Shoe Company. I look forward to hearing from you so that we can schedule an appointment at your earliest convenience.

Best Regards,

Susan Baker

Sample Cover Letter for an advertised CPA position:

GERALD SMITH, CPA
11 Skipper Ave. – Mid City, NJ 15372
Home: (555) 555-5555 Cell: (555) 555-5556 – gsmith@email.com

Nov. 20, 2009

Mr. Randy Jensen
Hiring Manager
Men's Fine Shoes
23 Shoe Blvd.

Mid City, NJ 19282

Dear Mr. Jensen:

As a **Certified Public Accountant** with over ten years of experience managing the books and taxes for small corporations, I believe you will find me the ideal candidate to meet your advertised needs. Highlights of my professional career include:

- Considerable experience in accounts receivable, billing, credit/collection, accounts payable, and accounting/financial Reporting, all for companies that employ 50 employees or less.

- Extensive tax preparation experience, including successful representation of five companies through IRS audits and finding ways to save new clients an average of 15 percent more than their previous accountants.

- Introduction of PC applications to automate accounting functions and increase data accuracy for payment billings at two companies.

After you have the opportunity to review my résumé, I would like to meet with you to discuss how I can effectively contribute to Men's Fine Shoes. I look forward to hearing from you so that we can schedule an appointment at your earliest convenience.

Best Regards,

Gerald Smith

Sample "Broadcast" Cover Letter for a Banking professional:

Angie Cunningham
10038 Gold Gate Drive – Chicago, IL 66830
(717) 555- 8728 – angiecunningham@email.com

September 24, 2009

David R. Duke
Recruiter
Bank of America
555 Bank of America Plaza
Chicago IL 67839

Dear Mr. Duke:

After the recent upheaval in the banking industry, I am sure you would appreciate a highly qualified banking professional with over 16 years of solid experience in positions of increasing responsibility and duties. If you are in need of such an individual, I have attached my résumé for your consideration.

In my years of experience, I have acquired a broad-based understanding of financial/banking needs at all levels of business. I am skilled in account management, sales management, customer service, marketing, branch management, loan administration, regulatory compliance, quality control, and teller operations. Throughout my career, I received recognition by management as a top performer for consistently achieving targeted sales goals and leading projects that have delivered profitable results and generated new business.

As a proven leader with excellent communication skills, I am proficient at motivating and training teams of professionals in meeting or exceeding identified company goals and customer expectations. With a proven track record of bringing in new customers and retaining existing accounts, I demonstrate excellent customer service and relationship-building skills.

I believe I can make an immediate contribution to Bank of America. If it appears that my qualifications meet your current needs, I would like to discuss those opportunities with you at greater length. I look forward to hearing from you to schedule an interview.

Respectfully,

Angie Cunningham

(This letter was written in Times New Roman at font size 11)

Administrative and Clerical Careers

Overall success: Focus on how your contributions have led to the overall success of your company. How have you increased productivity or efficiency? How have you reduced costs or managed projects?

Example:

As office assistant to a busy commercial real estate company, I reduced company costs by updating their e-communications, thus streamlining client communications.

Talk in depth: Discuss the size of the organizations for which you have been employed. Talk about the number of people you served and their varied backgrounds. Highlight your customer service skills as well.

Example:

> *As an administrative assistant, I provided clerical support and document management to 50 busy lawyers − full and junior partners − who specialized in tax, corporate, civil, and family law.*

Showcase your technical skills: From how fast you input data, to how many correct words per minute you can type, to which computer software programs you are proficient in − your technical skills are a vital resource to your potential employer.

Example:

> *Since both speed and accuracy are listed as your requirements, you would be served well by my ability to type 70 correct words per minute. Additionally, I am proficient in all Microsoft Office software, including Word, Excel, and PowerPoint.*

Keywords and phrases:

Administrative infrastructure	Budget and business administration
Back-office operations	Clerical support
Client communications	Confidential correspondence
Contract administration	Corporate record-keeping
Document management	Efficiency improvement
Front-office operations	Government affairs
Liaison affairs	Mail and messenger services
Meeting planning	Office management
Policy and procedure	Productivity improvement

Project management	Records management
Regulatory reporting	Resource management
Time management	Workflow planning/ prioritization

Sample Cover Letter for an advertised office assistant position:

ISAAC JOHNSON

P.O. Box 32882

Ocala FL 33333

(352) 555- 9839

Ijones80@email.com

Feb. 5th, 2009

Ms. Janie Brown

Atlantic Industries

jbrown@email.com

Dear Ms. Brown:

*I learned about your **office assistant** position through my job search on website.com. I am currently working as a customer service manager for an online paper supply company, but there is no room for advancement in this company at this time, so I am looking to branch out. I have attached my résumé for your review, as my skills appear to be a great match for your job opening.*

In my five years of employment with my current company, I assisted the owner significantly by handling all aspects of customer support and sales. One of my most rewarding experiences was when a large shipment to one of our customers failed to arrive on time. While it was not fun to deal with an understandably irate customer, it was my pleasure to track down their order and contact the shipping company to ensure that the customer received their order first thing the next day, which was in time for what they needed. I received a thank you letter from that manager for my diligence in customer service.

I am motivated by a drive to be excellent and a desire to see the company that I am working for prosper. I enjoy working in an office and performing administrative duties. I follow instructions to the letter, and I work late if a task needs extra effort to complete. Additionally, I am proficient in all Microsoft Office software, including Word, Excel, and PowerPoint.

I appreciate your time and consideration. I hope to meet with you to further discuss how I can be a valuable member of your team.

Sincerely,

Isaac Johnson

(This letter was written in Arial at font size 11).

Sample cover letter for an Administrative Assistant:

BRANDY WHITE
3928 West Vine Blvd.
City, State 39282
(283) 555-2920
bwhite@email.com

Feb. 21, 2009

Rich Hayes
North Eastern Press
rhayes@email.com

Dear Mr. Hayes:

I am submitting my résumé in response to your advertised listing for an **administrative assistant** in the City Daily. I have followed your company as one of the fasting growing companies in this area, and I would love to work for such a fast-paced, energetic organization.

I meet your listed qualifications in the following ways:

- As secretary of the City College's Student Government, I recorded and posted minutes for all meetings, transmitted communication between students, their government, and faculty sponsors, and prepared and sent a weekly e-newsletter demonstrating my ability to communicate information in an accurate, timely, and interesting way.

- Strong data entry skills learned working part-time as a research surveyor for the college's Government and Public Policy Department where I interviewed respondents at a 75 percent closure rating.

- Strong office skills including the ability to type 60 correct words per minute and proficiency in all Microsoft Office software including Word, Excel, PowerPoint, and Access as evidenced by high marks in related computer courses.

Your advertisement also stated that you expect applicants to be willing to work some nights and weekends. I have a strong work ethic and don't believe in slacking up just because the clock hits five. I think an interview would give us a better opportunity to ac-

cess if I am the perfect fit for this position. I will contact your office next week to schedule one at your earliest convenience. Thank you for your time and consideration.

Sincerely,

Brandy White

Sample cover letter for an advertised executive assistant position:

DONNA WILLIAMS

P.O. Box 33333 – Bayville, New Jersey 91823

Home: (354) 555-3922 Cell: (352) 555- 9839 – dwilliams@email.com

July 4, 2009

Ms. Sophia Dial
Fashion Forward
sdial@email.com

Dear Ms. Dial:

According to your advertisement on the Fashion Forward Web site, you need an executive assistant with a fine taste in fashion who is detail oriented and well organized. Please allow me to demonstrate why I am a perfect candidate by highlighting a few details from my attached résumé:

- *I have a dual degree in fashion design and business administration from State University, where I graduated with a 3.8 GPA.*

- *Five years experience as an administrative assistant at Women's Accessories Magazine, where I contribute to the successful production of the magazine through enabling efficient communication between departments, assisting page designers with layout, and assisting the chief editor with her column and content decisions.*

- *My most rewarding experiences have been working with the magazine photographers on the coordination of models' ensembles to highlight the accessories in our magazines.*

Working for you at Fashion Forward would be a thrilling advancement in this industry. I read your magazine monthly to pick up on hot tips for my wardrobe, but what I love about Fashion Forward is your dedication to charitable causes and your focus on making fashion less materialistic and more fun.

I am an energetic employee whose attention to detail has been noted by supervisors and professors. I bring a drive to excel at everything I do in life. On the technical front, I am experienced in all Microsoft Office software, including Word, Excel, Access, and PowerPoint. Also, I am accustomed to operating a multi-phone line system and can type over 60 correct words per minute.

I hope to meet with you to further discuss how I can be a valuable member of your team and will follow up with you in ten days to schedule an interview. Thank you for your time and consideration.

Sincerely,

Donna Williams

(This letter was written in Arial at font size 11)

Sample Cover Letter for an Office Administrator posted with an online résumé:

Trisha Smith
301 West Peach Tree St.
Atlanta, GA 48273
(797) 555-9484

Dear Sir/Ma'am:

After working 12 years for a small, family-run insurance company, I find myself looking for new employment. The wonderful owner passed away and the family has decided not to continue the business he started. I worked as his bookkeeper and administrative assistant from the time I graduated with my bachelor's from the University of Georgia until now.

While his passing is a great loss for me, it is with excitement that I embark on my quest for a new job. I am detailed oriented, keeping perfect books the entire time I worked at my current position (which held up to the close scrutiny of an IRS audit in 2002). I am an excellent multitasker, managing my duties as a mother of two boys and my employer's busy office schedule. I'm a self-starter who doesn't need to be asked to fill a need — I simply get things done.

My résumé is listed detailing my skills and accomplishments, but I would enjoy speaking with any interested parties in greater length about how I can assist their office like I did for so many years for my former employer.

Regards,

Trisha Smith

(This letter was written in Times New Roman at font size 12)

Sample Cover Letter for a Staff Assistant:

AMANDA VICKS

77 Cornerstone Blvd.

City, State 45282

(342) 555-2920

avicks@email.com

Sept. 21, 2009

Stacey McRoy

Executive Assistant

smcroy@email.com

Dear Ms. McRoy

*I am submitting my résumé in response to your advertised listing for a **junior staff assistant** on www.website.com. As a recent graduate, my education and experience make me an ideal fit for this entry-level position.*

I meet your listed qualifications in the following ways:

- *A four-year degree in business administration.*

- *Two years experience as secretary in the Career Counselors office at State University where I increased my correct word-per-minute count to 65 and became proficient in all Microsoft Office software including Word, Excel, Power-Point, and Outlook.*

- *One year's experience as secretary in the Financial Aid office at City Community College where I received phone calls, e-mails, and faxes and channeled them to the right personnel dealing with time sensitive and confidential material in a professional and accurate manner.*

- *Excellent customer service skills learned in both positions as I assisted students with their needs.*

An interview would demonstrate to you how well I would fit in your office and I hope to schedule one with you in the near future. I will contact you next week to find your earliest possible opening. Thank you for your time and consideration. I look forward to meeting with you soon.

Respectfully,

Amanda Vicks

(This cover letter was written in Arial at font size 11)

Sample Cover Letter for Director of Admissions:

Jane Smith
5555 Belle Avenue
Davenport, IA 55555
(563) 555-8858

June 25, 2009

Susan Smith, Ph.D.
Director Office of Academic Affairs
Hebrew University of Jerusalem
Rothberg International School
One Battery Park Plaza
New York, NY 55555

Dear Dr. Alperstein:

There's no place like home! After taking my junior year abroad at Rothberg, spending a semester as a visiting grad student, completing both Arabic and Hebrew summer plans, and earning my Master's at the Rothberg International School, I do consider Rothberg my academic home. The school means a great deal to me.

I expect that you may be hard pressed to find a candidate for the position of assistant director of admissions in the New York office who personally knows Rothberg's programs and how much can be gained from them as well as I do. As an alumna from the programs listed above, I know from first-hand experience what issues, concerns, and roadblocks students and students' families are likely to encounter before they leave for the program, while they are there, and after they come back. I believe that my experiences have taught me how to handle them smoothly. On the Israeli side of the program, in the three and a half years I spent at Rothberg, I came to know most of the administrative staff on a first name basis.

As you can see from my résumé, I have considerable experience, both in the field of market research, where I worked for a market research firm for two and a half years, and in administrative duties.

I look forward to discussing this opportunity with you in person. I look forward to hearing from you so we can schedule an interview. Thank you very much.

Sincerely,

Jane Smith

(This letter was prepared by contributor Shira Karp)

Computer Engineering and IT Careers

Continuing Education: If you have any certifications, or further education in your field, make sure to make mention of them in your cover letter. IT is a field that evolves more rapidly than almost any other. Innovations that were cutting edge two years ago may now be obsolete. Be sure to list any classes or training that conveys that you have kept abreast of technology.

Technical Achievements: Technology is an industry where the deliverables are constantly being measured. If you managed to complete a software project ahead of schedule, develop something unique, or refine a process that allowed your company to save or make money, be sure to highlight it. This is especially important in careers in technical support. Whether you work internal or external support, your ability to handle and resolve issues is vital to the success of any organization.

Teamwork: If you have worked in technology, chances are, you were part of the team. Relate how you helped your team or organization achieve its goals. In this age of technology, the IT structure is often the backbone of most organizations. If the servers or workstations stop working, everyone stops working. A good IT group will prevent this from happening. Let your audience know how well you have interacted with your fellow team members and how valuable you are or were to their organization.

Customer Service: People know you are good with computers, technology and software, but if you want to show them your diversity, assure them of your customer service skills. A hiring authority will want to know that you have the ability to explain to others (be it customers or fellow staff) the services you provide in plain, easy to understand terminology.

Training Experience: In the same vein as your customer service skills, you may be expected to train your company on new software. Your ability to advance in your career may depend on your talent as a trainer. Show the hiring authority that you can effectively communicate instructions to others, and you may distinguish yourself from your peers.

Review the keywords and phrases on the following page:

Keywords and phrases for **Computer Engineering and IT Professionals**:

Applications development	Artificial intelligence
Automated voice response	Benchmarking
Broadband	Certifications
Client/server architecture	Computer science
Cross-functional technology team	Customer service
Data center operations	Data communications
Data recovery	Database administration
Database design	Database server
Desktop technology	Disaster recovery
Document imaging	Electronic data interchange
Emerging technologies	End-user support
Enterprise systems	Fault analysis
Field support	Firewall
Geographical information system (GIS)	Global systems support
Graphical user interface (GUI)	Hardware configuration
Hardware development/ engineering	Host-based system
Internet	Joint application development (JAD)

Just-in-time (JIT)	Local-area network (LAN)
Mainframe	Management information systems
Multimedia technology	Multiuser interface
Multi-vendor systems integration	Network administration
Object-orientated programming	Office automation
Operating system	Parallel systems operations
Pilot implementation	Project management
Rapid application development	Remote systems access
Research and development	Satellite communications
Software configuration	Software Development Life Cycle (SDLC)
Software development/ engineering	Systems analysis and design
Systems configuration	Systems development
Systems engineering	Systems implementation
Systems integration	Systems security
Technical documentation and writing	Technical training and licensing
Technical solutions and transfer	Thin/Thick client
User training and support	World Wide Web

Sample Cover Letter to a Headhunter for a Computer Engineer:

Ron Mayer

2384 Line Blvd. — Big City, CA 98373 — (978) 555 - 5344

May 1, 2009

Franklin Smith
Solutions Management
fsmith@email.com

Dear Mr. Smith,

I would like to take the time to introduce myself and possibly engage your services in my procurement of new employment. I am looking for a position that would benefit from my 13 years of experience in the IT field, which includes desktop support, large WAN administration, and quality control for various software applications.

I have, at various times in my career, managed teams ranging from four to twelve employees to complete date-sensitive projects. I feel I can be a valuable resource to any company that sees fit to employ my services, and I have a proven track record of being a very loyal and hard working member of whatever organization I am a part of.

My extensive technological background began with my B.S. degree in computer engineering from ACME University, with a minor in operations management. From there, I worked for a large robotics corporation, J-Five Alive Corp. I started in their desktop support team, primarily telling users to stop using their CD-ROM trays as coffee cup holders. I later worked on the network administration team after several years and was placed in charge of maintaining the western region's network of servers.

My next job was at a software company that found my experience with networking appealing, but also found my operations management background a must. I was placed in charge of the IT support personnel and we maintained a network of approximately 12 servers and 150 or so workstations. I was promoted from IT manager to the quality assurance manager after five years, and took part in ensuring that the software that company released was as bug-free and stable as possible. In addition to managing the team, I wrote the testing scripts, and outlined the metrics for our QA staff. We achieved a 96 percent error free score on our software releases dur-

ing my tenure, an achievement I am extremely proud of.

Due to a need to relocate, I am now in need of a position in your area. My salary range is $65,000-$75,000. I hope to hear from you soon and learn more about your clientele who may find my résumé appealing.

Regards,

Ron Mayer

Sample Cover Letter for an advertisement for a Computer Software professional:

JENNIFER JONES

4422 Smith Street   *(456) 555-6490*
Baton Rouge, LA 49830   *jjones@email.com*

April 13, 2009

Mr. Fred Smart
Gulf Coast Mortgages
Fax: (456) 555- 3937

Dear Mr. Smart:

With 14 years of experience in various coding methodologies and languages, I will design your core payment processing system in a way that is both user-friendly and dependable. I worked as an assistant manager for five years at Radio Shack as I earned a dual degree in computer engineering and business administration. In that time, I consistently led my store in sales proving my ability to relate effectively to customers.

My additional qualifications include:

- *My second job out of college was for a software company whose products monitored and audited large credit card transactions for major retailers. I gained a great deal of experience in ACH systems and protocols in this position.*

- *I am well versed with Java and other OO related programming. One of my Java-related projects involved developing a thin client that was essentially a web based wrapper around one of our product interfaces.*

- *My excellent writing skills were honed in my work as a technical writer, having produced several of the manuals that have accompanied a slew of our products.*

- *At my current job, I was lead developer on several projects, and I architected the backend SQL database for our data warehousing software.*

I meet deadlines early and pride myself as a colleague that my co-workers can both rely and lean on. I believe that a good leader sets an example and is an encouraging voice in the work environment. I look forward to meeting with you to discuss how my skills can immediately serve your needs.

Respectfully,

Jennifer Jones

(This letter was written in Bookman Old Style at font size 10)

Editing, Journalism, Public Relations, and Communications Careers

Show strong writing skills: Your cover letter — more than any-one else's — will need to be impeccably written. You are a writer by trade, and as such, you should demonstrate a command of the written word in your submission. You must make sure your letter is free of typos and grammatical mistakes.

Show diversity: Journalism professionals should demonstrate the wide range of writing experience they possess by referenc-ing the different styles of writing they have performed. Have you covered hard news, political beats, feature articles, sports, or written a column?

As a public relations professional, you should showcase the wide range of products, companies, or people you have represented. Have you worked for a campaign (grassroots or paid)? What types of products have you represented? What types of compa-nies did you represent? Have you worked for clients that really needed help with their public image?

Work environment: Journalism professionals should discuss the paper or magazine for which they write. Did you work at a weekly or a daily? Are you used to hard deadlines? What is the circulation of the papers for which you worked?

Public relations professionals should discuss the size and diver-sity of the companies and/or products they have represented.

Skills other than writing: Did you take pictures, work on layout, or do page designs? What computer programs are you familiar with?

Consider the keywords and phrases for **Journalism and Public Relations Professionals**:

Advertising communications	Agency relations
Brand management and strategy	Broadcast and print media
Campaign management	Community affairs and outreach
Competitive market lead	Conference planning
Corporate identity and advertising	Corporate communications
Corporate sponsorship	Corporate vision
Creative services	Crisis and customer communications
Direct-mail campaign	Electronic advertising and media
Employee communications	Event management
Fund-raising	Government relations
Grass-roots campaign	Investor communications
Issues management	Legislative affairs
Management communications	Market research
Marketing communications	Media buys and placement
Media relations	Media scheduling
Meeting planning	Merchandising
Multimedia advertising	Political Action Committee (PAC)
Premiums	Press releases
Promotions	Public relations and speaking
Publications	Publicity
Sales incentives	Shareholder communication
Strategic communications plan	Strategic planning and positioning
Tactical campaign	VIP relations

Sample Cover Letter for a Newspaper Manager written to accompany an online résumé posting:

Charles Harold "Harry" Madison

P.O. Box 3728 — Atlanta, GA 38921 — Tel. (607) 555-4868

To Potential Employers:

I am writing to express interest in a newspaper management position that you may be seeking to fill.

With over 25 years of experience as an editor and journalist, I believe I have the qualifications you are seeking.

My years in the newspaper industry include six years I spent as the publisher and editor of my own community weekly in Alabama. The paper was established in the early 1900s, but by 1996 when I purchased the company, it was in a distressed condition, both in coverage and business operations. Under my leadership, we turned the situation around, and I sold the paper in 2002 for 50 percent above the purchase price.

Prior to that, I worked eight years as the top editor and manager of a news department in Mobile. My column was widely read and the paper increased its circulation by 25 percent during my time there. I trained the reporters that worked under me with diligence and high standards. Three of them now manage news rooms themselves for newspapers with circulations over 150,000.

After selling the weekly in 2002 and moving to Atlanta, I began a teaching career at the Peach Tree Charter High School in their remarkable journalism program. It has been my pleasure to be the faculty advisor for the student-run newspaper and guide these budding writers in all aspects of AP Style, sports reporting, and editing. However, now that my youngest child has graduated high school, I find myself longing again for the newsroom.

I have substantial experience with daily, semi-weekly, and weekly newspapers and total-market-coverage shopper publications, as my posted résumé will further detail. I am an enthusiastic leader with substantial training and teaching experience. I am a cool-headed consensus builder and pride myself on being an effective motivator and problem solver. I have spent years adapting quickly to an ever-changing business, and I work diligently to get the job done right.

My newsroom philosophy is: A newspaper should be satisfied with nothing less than the constant improvement of itself and the community it serves.

If you feel that I have the experience and skills you require, I would like very much to discuss the job with you. I look forward to hearing from you.

Sincerely,

Harry

(This letter was written in Times New Roman at font size 11.5)

Sample Cover Letter from a recent college graduate for staff writer:

PETER DORING_____
282 Main Street
Capitol, State 22911
(382) 555-3922
pdoring@email.com

May 1, 2009

Mr. Julian Berger
Managing Editor
Florida Press
jberger@email.com

Dear Mr. Berger:

As a recent college graduate with a B.S. in journalism from the University of Florida who also possesses a great deal of writing experience, I would like to be considered for your open staff writer position. My attached résumé and writing samples will demonstrate in detail my qualifications, but I would like to point out a few highlights here, including:

- Seven years of experience writing for student publications starting my sophomore year of high school, continuing through community college, and onto contributions to The Gator Press at UF. My greatest accomplishment came when I published an in-depth investigative report on the food quality at the dinners at my community college. This led to the college changing out providers and the significant improvement in the quality of food provided.

- Two years of editing experience for student publications, my senior year high school paper, and my second year working on the community college newspaper.

- Four years of freelance experience, ranging from sports coverage to feature articles in two city publications with circulations over 50,000.

- *An exciting internship at the Orlando Sentinel where I spent 12-hour days copywriting countless stories.*

I would enjoy meeting with you to further discuss whether I am the right fit for your office. I look forward to hearing from you in the near future to schedule an interview.

Sincerely,

Karen Thomas

Sample Cover letter for an advertised Editorial Assistant position:

SAMATHA ROBERTSON

1000 SW Orange Street – Sacramento, California 97844
966-555-7653 – slrobertson73@email.com

May 14, 2009

Robert Henderson
West Coast Publishing
rhenderson@email.com

Dear Mr. Henderson:

My experience writing for a large Washington business journal and other various publications, including a British punk music magazine, makes me the ideal candidate for becoming your **editorial assistant***.*

My time at the Seattle Business Journal was an amazing experience. While working under editor-in-chief Michelle Smith, I honed my proofing and editing skills and cultivated my own sources and stories. The majority of my stay was spent copyediting other writers' work and doing research for stories on business developments in Seattle. However, Ms. Smith became so confident in my abilities that I was allowed to pursue some of my own profiles and feature story ideas as well.

Having my byline printed in such a prestigious Washington publication was a thrill I will never forget. I attached two writing samples from my work there, along with my résumé to this e-mail.

My other work history includes:

- *Editorial Assistant for Big Ben Magazine in London. The magazine is one of the U.K.'s leading alternative music magazines. While working at the small, four-man editorial office, I wrote features and album, movie, concert, and book reviews on a daily basis. I also promoted every new issue by going online and scouring Web sites and fan pages to get the word out; in addition, I cultivated some contacts in Australia to help expand the magazine overseas.*

- *Freelance reporter for the Sacramento Star, where I started my career. The Star has a circulation of around 70,000. My time was spent mostly covering local high school sporting events, including feature articles on several of the coaches and student athletes.*

Thank you for your time and consideration. I would love to meet with you to discuss how I can make an immediate positive impact on your company. I look forward to speaking with you so we can schedule an interview.

Respectfully,

Samantha Robertson

(This letter was written in Tahoma in font size 10)

Sample Cover Letter for an Editorial Assistant:

JOSEPH FLOYD
55 Ivy Court
Davenport, IA 52807
(563) 555-3892

February 24, 2009

Nicole Matthews
Senior Editor
Publishing House, Inc.
1745 Broadway
New York, NY 10019

Dear Ms. Matthews:

*Being fluent in French, German, Spanish, and Russian, I believe you will find my language skills extremely useful as your international **editorial assistant**, which was advertised on the Publishing House Web site. I have attached my résumé for your review.*

I am a recent graduate from a master's program in International Relations at Columbia. As a student of political and social sciences, I research, write, and edit a large number of papers on a variety of topics. I have over two years of administrative background and two years of experience working for my community's newspaper. In high school, I was very actively involved in my school's yearbook and newspaper, in addition to being editor-in-chief of the school's literary magazine. I believe my varied background and interests will prove an asset to your publishing firm.

I am a creative, motivated candidate who is organized and able to multi-task. I love a challenge and am used to working under deadlines. Through my extensive work on research papers for my degrees and various customer service oriented jobs, I have developed exceptional written and oral communication skills. As an avid reader, I would bring a personal passion to the job.

Thank you for your time and consideration. I will be in New York in two weeks visiting family and hope to speak with you at that time. I will call Monday to schedule an appointment per your availability.

Respectfully,

Joseph Floyd

(This letter was prepared by contributor Shira Karp)

Sample Cover Letter to a Headhunter for a Public Relations officer:

Vivian "Vicky" George

282 Lee Street   (432) 555-9382
Capitol, State 29382   vgeorge@email.com

April 21, 2009

Christopher Langley
81559 State St.
Capitol, State 21361

Dear Mr. Langley:

If your clientele need a bottom-line results focused representative with over 12 years success as a public relations director, I would enjoy meeting with them. Having served corporations such as Bank USA, Southwestern Telecom and American Computer Software, my success at enhancing a company's public image is phenomenal.

Since my current employer is merging with another company, I am exploring new employment opportunities. Please allow me to highlight some of the details from my attached résumé:

- *Excellent campaign strategy demonstrated through the effective launch of Web sites, ad campaigns, product launches, and logo redesign.*

- *Leadership qualities shown by motivating team members and empowering them to take action rather than come to me for approval on every issue.*

- *Success at juggling multiple projects at once while giving each of them the attention they deserve.*

- *A track record of initiatives that result in increased awareness and press coverage, successful advertising campaigns, and winning branding strategies.*

I desire to stay on the West Coast and am looking for a salary in the range of $80,000-$100,000. I am well aware that many companies have their own "culture" and that a highly qualified candidate is not always the perfect person for the job. Therefore, I would like to meet with you so you can get a better feel for my personality and which of your clients I would best serve. I will be in your area next Thursday and would like to schedule an interview for that day if you have an open time. I will contact you on Monday in this regards.

Respectfully,

Vickie George

Sample Cover Letter from a recent college graduate for assistant editor:

KAREN THOMAS

4559 S. Tennessee Ave.

Lake, Fl 33801

KSThomasFL@email.com

(432) 555-3843

Dear Mr. Julian Webb:

*As a recent college graduate with a B.S. in Communication from the University of South Florida, I understand why you might not consider me a strong candidate for your **assistant editor** opening. However, my résumé should demonstrate to you that I received more than just an education in my time at USF − I received practical hands on experience that makes me competitive in today's difficult job market.*

Any writer will tell you they have a passion for the written word. I want to show you more than my passion − I want to show you that I can do the job as well as my competitors who might have more professional experience than I do.

To meet that goal, let me highlight a few aspects of my attached résumé:

- *I wrote and edited for the campus newspaper. As a student reporter, I published in-depth investigative reports on the counseling that victims of date-rape were receiving at our campus. The series of articles won national honors at the college newspaper convention last year.*

- *The summer of 2008, I interned at the Chicago Times. I was one of a dozen interns selected to work in one of the busiest newsrooms in the country. I spent 12-hour days copywriting countless stories. At the end of my internship, my supervisor, Jack Brown, said my work was incredible and he would gladly serve as a professional reference for me.*

- *I worked on the college's online newspaper for course credit last fall. In this course, I learned about page layout, web-design, and HTML. Besides writing original content, I also wrote all headlines and photo captions for the paper. It was an invaluable experience as it made me confident I can handle online duties in the area of Internet news.*

I would enjoy meeting with you to further discuss whether I am the right fit for your office. I look forward to hearing from you in the near future to schedule an interview.

Sincerely,

Karen Thomas

Government Careers

Security clearance: Any government careers will require you to have a security clearance. If you have one already — mention it in your cover letter. If you do not currently have one, mention your confidence at being able to obtain one.

Other documents: Government jobs will often require you to have documentation other than a security clearance. This may include statements of Key Skill Areas, answers to specific questions, and information about particular skills, such as language proficiencies. Go ahead and give these details in your cover letter where possible, or mention an enclosure where needed.

Military experience: Many government jobs will give favored status to applicants with a military background. Point out your military experience by using an example from your career in the armed forces to showcase your job skills.

Keywords and phrases:

Briefings and trainings	Budget planning and allocation
Congressional affairs	Cross-cultural communication
Cultural diversity	Foreign government relations
Government affairs	Inter-agency relations
International trade and commerce	Legislative affairs
Liaison affairs	Lobbying
Press relations and media affairs	Procurement and acquisitions
Program design and management	Public advocacy
Public works	Regulatory reporting
SEC affairs	Zoning and compliance

Cover Letter Sample for Government job:

Jessica Langley
2827 Downing Avenue – Little City, TN 29282
(293) 555-9282 – Jessica.langley@email.com

Mayor Tammy Moore
Town of Sister City

100 Main Street.
Sister City, Tenn 38272

Dear Mayor Moore:

During my 11-year career as a public official, I have acquired broad experience and honed diverse skills that I believe will be of interest to the town of Sister City. My background, detailed in the attached résumé, demonstrates that I possess the necessary strategic planning and financial, project, and people management skills to qualify me to serve as your community's town administrator.

What do I offer?

- *More than 11 years experience as the Public Works officer for the town of Little City.*

- *More than 20 years experience as a small business owner.*

- *Proactive leadership with proven ability to inspire cooperation, communication, and consensus among personnel and other groups.*

- *Development and administration of a $10 million budget, as well as planning and overseeing multiple projects to meet community needs.*

- *Contributing to economic development by building strong public/private partnerships and negotiating agreements.*

Examples of my accomplishments:

- *Planning and implementing the extension of the town's sewer and water lines to facilitate growth and expansion.*

- *Budgeting for a water and sewer impact fee moratorium the city implemented during a harsh economic period to stimulate growth.*

- *Sound fiscal management that improved benefit programs without cost increases.*

This position as town administrator is exciting to me for many reasons including the ability to move back to my hometown and enjoy the company of my aging parents and extended family. I will be visiting that family in two weeks and hope to meet with you at that time. I will call you in a couple of days to schedule an interview.

Best regards,

Jessica Langley

(This letter was written in Arial at font size 10)

Sample cover letter for Congressional job:

SUSAN SMITH

73 Pine Street – Washington D.C. 21039

(693) 555-0939 – ssmith@email.com

May 10, 2009

Helen Martinez
Chief of Staff
Congressman John Jones' Office
hmartinez@email.com

Dear Ms. Martinez:

Sarah Richardson informed me that Congressman Jones is looking for a **staff assistant** in his Washington D.C. office and suggested that I send you my résumé with her referral. As you know, Ms. Richardson is one of the Congressman's greatest supporters. She and my mother grew up together in Florida's 7th District. My mother was thrilled when Congressman Jones ran for election, and I remember holding a sign with her on Election Day when I was seven.

Despite an early predisposition to love the Congressman, I came to admire him for my own reasons as I graduated from high school and attended State University. I am proud of his efforts to improve the local economy and serve as a strong voice for education. It would be an honor to work for Congressman Jones to help him fulfill his agenda in Washington.

Highlights from my attached résumé include:

- Graduation with a B.S. in Political Science in 2007.

- An internship as a research assistant with the Republican National Committee in 2006. While at the RNC, I supported many state and national campaigns by preparing extensive research reports and writing issue summaries for candidates and campaign staff.

- An initiative campaign in Florida where I conducted research for press releases, collected and organized donations, prepared speech material for the grassroots representatives throughout the state, and fielded voter concerns as one of several people who answered the phones. The initiative was successfully passed in Nov. 2008.

- *A six-month internship with the American Heart Association in their lobbying department in Washington D.C. where I have meet with a number of Capitol Hill figures.*

With ties to Congressman Jones' community and the necessary skills to serve in this position, I believe I am an ideal candidate. After you review my résumé, I am sure you will agree that I can make a positive contribution to the Congressman's office. Thank you for your consideration. I will follow up with you next week to schedule a time to meet.

Sincerely,

Susan Smith

(This letter is written in Tahoma at font size 11)

Sample cover letter for a city's Chief Financial Officer:

Ayla Sarmiento

199 Pony Lane — Glen Burnie MD 21089

(410) 555-9282 — aylasarmiento@email.com

May 1, 2009

Brandy Lohsl
City of Lakeland
9000 City Blvd.
Lakeland FL 38272

Dear Ms. Lohsl:

Throughout my 25-year career, I displayed both strong business management expertise and the unique ability to build consensus among diverse political and special interest groups to cooperate toward common goals. With extensive experience working for the highest levels of government and on high-profile cross-agency projects, I demonstrated outstanding leadership skills and the ability to manage extensive, diverse responsibilities. All of these skills make me an idea candidate as your city's Chief Financial Officer.

With a bachelor's degree in political science and an MBA, I began my career in campaign finance working for a congressional campaign. Since that time, I have had the opportunity to work for several elected officials and government departments. My enclosed résumé will fully detail my skills and achievements, but please allow me to highlight some here:

- Strategic planning that facilitated departmental vision by committing to action and achieving goals in the most efficient and effective manner.

- Building high-performance, cross-disciplinary teams vital to overall project management and product delivery.

- Contributing actively to team projects by working with peers and colleagues and collaborating on solutions.

- Budgeting skills that were adaptable and flexible as unforeseen issues arose.

I would like to meet with you to discuss how I can make an immediate positive contribution to your city. I look forward to hearing from you.

Sincerely,

Ayla Sarmiento

FRANKLIN DONALD "DONNY" SMITH
181 Rosewood Court – City, State 19822
(329) 555-2928 – fds3357@email.com

March 3, 2009

Mr. Harold Jones
US Department of Energy
Executive and Technical Resources
555 Independence Avenue, SW
Washington, D.C. 55555

ATTN: ETR-02-ES-007

Dear Mr. Jones:

This letter transmits my application for the position of human resource assistant director (EV- 0340/01). Enclosed you will find my résumé, Executive Success Profile, and KSA narratives, constituting all information requested by the announcement.

As a senior executive human resource manager with over 25 years of success in the industry, I will make an immediate contribution to your team. Highlighted in greater detail in my résumé, my relevant qualifications include:

- *Detailed employment law knowledge: EEO, OSHA, COBRA, FMLA, ERISA, ADA, and FLSA.*

- *High proficiency directing state-of-the-art policy development and operational human resource management programs.*

- *Active "Q" Security Clearance.*

- *Proven successful experience leading change, including streamlining hiring practices for several companies, as well as implementing employee evaluation processes that increased satisfaction by an average of 15 percent.*

- *Special talent for building, retaining, and motivating knowledgeable and efficient management and workforce teams with a productivity rating of 100 percent.*

- *Expertise in workforce planning, staffing and recruitment, compensation, labor and employee relations, and training and associated automated personnel systems.*

Thank you for your time and consideration. I look forward to meeting with you to further discuss my application. I will call you later in the week to set up an interview at your earliest convenience.

Respectfully,

Donny Smith

Cover Letter Sample for Government job:

Melissa Anderson

2823 Fifth Avenue — Little City, FL. 39282
(352) 555-9282 — Melissa.Anderson@email.com

Mayor Eric Long
Town of Lady Lake
100 Main Street
Lady Lake, FL 38272

Dear Mayor Long:

Ten years ago I left the corporate world to work for a non-profit organization close to my heart. After my mother was diagnosed with lung cancer, I dedicated myself to the American Heart and Lung Association. A month after she died, I received a job offer to work full-time as the human resource director for the state of Florida.

In three months I will relocate to Lady Lake to help my sister look after her children. Because of my need to assist her I am looking for a local job opportunity. I saw your advertisement for a department head of human resources on the city's Web site. After reviewing your stated requirements, I believe we are a perfect fit.

My enclosed résumé details my skills and accomplishments, but I would like to take the time to tell you about one of the greatest joys of my career. Two years ago the American Lung Association in Florida was interviewing for a state lobbyist. We went through a long list of candidates without finding the perfect fit for the position. Then a recent graduate from the campaigning program at the University of Florida walked into our office. She was young and only had an internship and a couple of small volunteer campaigns on her résumé, but she showed a passion for our cause and we decided to take a chance on her. After one year in Tallahassee, she pushed forward our agenda with better results than any other lobbyist had done in the decade I worked with the organization.

I tell you this story to illustrate both that I understand the importance of finding the "right fit" for your office and that I have a fine eye for finding that fit. I would like to meet with you to discuss further what I can do for you in this position. I will contact you next week to schedule an interview.

Sincerely,

Melissa Anderson

(This cover letter was written in Arial at font size 10)

Healthcare and Social Services Careers

Patients/Clients: Showcase your diversity by talking about the volume and diversity of patients or clients you have treated or served.

Skills: Be sure to mention relevant healthcare procedures you can perform or equipment you can operate.

List Credentials: Do this by listing the appropriate initials after your name in your contact information or spelling out your licenses or certifications and placing them near the top of your letter. This is critical information, and something your reader will be looking to see immediately.

Be on the cutting edge: Discuss any involvement you have had in research or the development and/or introduction of new procedures or techniques. Any exposure to new treatments and protocols could be a point of interest to a hiring director.

Keywords and phrases:

Acute care facility	Ambulatory care
Assisted living	Behavior modification
Capital giving campaign	Case management
Certificate of need (CON)	Chronic care facility
Client advocacy	Clinical services
Community hospital	Community outreach
Continuity of care	Cost center
Crisis intervention	Diagnostic evaluation and intervention
Electronic claims processing	Emergency medical systems (EMS)

Employee assistance programs	Free billing
Full-time equivalent	Grant administration
Health-care administrator	Health-care delivery systems
Health maintenance organization (HMO)	Home health care
Hospital foundation	Human services
Industrial medicine	Inpatient and outpatient care
Insurance administration	Integrated service delivery
Long-term care and managed care	Management service organization (MSO)
Multi-hospital network	Occupation health
Patient accounting	Patient and provider relations
Peer review	Physician credentials
Physician relations	Practice management
Preferred provider organization (PPO)	Preventative medicine
Primary care	Protective services
Public health administration	Regulatory affairs and reporting
Risk management	Vocational rehabilitation

Sample cover letter for a recent graduate to an advertised position for a Pharmaceutical researcher:

ROBERT "ROB" PATTERSON
392 W. First Street — Knoxville, TN 20291
rpatterson@email.com — (493) 555-2894

July 5, 2009

R. Langley
Hiring Manager
ABC Drugs
rlangley@email.com

RE: Staffing, Job Code: LMN-ZOE-RC

Dear R. Langley:

In response to your advertisement on website.com, I am attaching my résumé for your review for the position of **research associate**. ABC Drugs has a reputation for being on the cutting edge of pharmaceutical development including patented cancer and AIDs treatments. After watching my father die of cancer in high school, working for a company that contributes to the treatment and most especially pain management of cancer patients has been my goal.

I graduated from State University in May 2007 with a Bachelor of Science Degree. My major was chemical and pharmaceutical engineering. As you will see from my résumé, in addition to meeting the demands of a full-time academic schedule and carrying a 3.7 GPA, I worked as a lab assistant throughout my time at State. This experience gave me the opportunity to work closely with department professors as they conducted their academic research for conferences and publications.

My education, experience, and passion make me an ideal candidate for this position. I would like to meet with you at ABC Drugs so we can further discus the immediate positive impact I can make in your research department. I look forward to hearing from you to schedule an interview at your earliest convenience. Thank you very much for your time and any consideration.

Sincerely,

Rob Patterson

Cover Letter Sample for Healthcare professional:

JENNIFER ANDERSON
Licensed Nursing Home Administrator
229 Spring Hill Road — Livingston SC 28272
(737) 555-8270 — janderson@email.com

September 10, 2009

Lauren J. Jones, MD
President and CEO
Blue Lake Plaza
2827 Blue Lake Blvd.
Land-o-Lakes, SC 38727

Dear Ms. Jones:

Amanda Logan asked that I forward my résumé to you in consideration for the executive director position with Blue Lake Inc. She indicated that she visited with you about my qualifications and that you would be expecting my letter. It is with great interest and enthusiasm that I submit the enclosed information.

Briefly stated, my credentials include:

- *Current licensure in the states North and South Carolina as a Nursing Home Administrator, Registered Nurse, and Registered Dietician.*

- *Ten years of Continuing Care Retirement Community experience in managerial, administrative, and leadership roles guiding a team of 100 plus members.*

- *Registered nurse with extensive background in emergency room, outpatient surgery, and surgical units.*

- *Five years experience as a registered dietician.*

The attached résumé outlines in greater detail my background and experience in the nursing home administrative profession. I would be happy to share more details with you, and I look forward to scheduling a meeting to do so. I appreciate your consideration and look forward to hearing from you.

Sincerely,

Jennifer Anderson

Sample cover letter for an advertised position for a Medical Equipment Tester:

WILLIAM "BILL" GAMBREL
29 Second Street
Knoxville, TN 20291
billg@email.com
(493) 555-2894

April 21, 2009

Mr. Christian Langley
Hiring Director
Medical Equipment Labs
clangley@email.com

Dear Mr. Langley:

*In response to your advertisement on website.com, I am attaching my résumé for your review for the position of **medical equipment tester**. I have watched with great interest as your company has produced industry equipment since my sister was first fitted with a hearing aid from your company when she was six years old. I was fourteen at the time, and the joy on her face when she could hear clearly because of your device left a lifetime impression. I now hope to be part of the team that makes such innovative technology available to little girls like her.*

I graduated from the University of Tennessee with a Bachelor of Science Degree majoring in medical science last year. As you can see from my attached résumé, in addition to my studies, in which I carried a 3.9 GPA, I gained hands-on experience by being a research assistant for Dr. Philip Matthews and through an internship at Southern Labs.

My experience and enthusiasm makes me an excellent candidate for the position you are seeking to fill. I would like to meet with you at Medical Equipment Labs so that I can further demonstrate what I can offer to the company. I look forward to hearing from you to schedule an interview at your earliest convenience. Thank you very much for your time and any consideration.

Sincerely,

Bill Gambrel

Sample cover letter for an occupational therapist:

KATIE BELLE

1817 Lime Street — Pittsburg PA 28271

Katiebelle80@email.com — (372) 555-9283

April 2, 2009

Ms. Jean O'Brian
HR Director
Comfort Care Learning Center
700 Breeze Hwy.
Pittsburg, PA 28273

Dear Ms. O'Brian:

As a well-trained, and competent occupational therapist with eight years of experience — focusing on work with children in the school setting — I believe I am someone who will be an asset to your firm. With solid skills and a proven record of success in assessing children's OT needs and developing and executing targeted treatment plans, I would like you to consider putting my talents and expertise to work as a part of your staff.

As you can see from my enclosed résumé, my last three years have been spent entirely with young children — ranging in ages from two to five. I provided services in both public and private schools and daycare facilities during that time. I addressed and treated a broad range of needs while accumulating a wealth of knowledge and expertise.

The keys of my success include solid training and up-to-date therapeutic skills. I partner well with teachers and receive exceptional feedback from parents due to my ability to communicate with them regarding their children's needs.

With the caring, nurturing service I provide, you can be confident that I will be an asset to your organization and your students. I would be pleased to discuss future employment with you and hope *to have an opportunity to meet with you on this matter. Thank you for your consideration.*

Sincerely,

Katie Belle

Hospitality and Food Service Careers

Cuisine: Make mention of the types of cuisine you are familiar with. If you are a chef — what types of food do you specialize in preparing? If you are a server — what types of food are you knowledgeable about? What types of wine are you familiar with?

Establishments: Have you worked for a four-star restaurant? What is the size of the hotel chain for which you have been employed? Does that chain have a quality rating? What type of facilities did they feature (for example: spa, golf course, or tennis club)?

Guests/Patrons: Discuss the diversity and number of guests or patrons you served. Did you work for a busy, large restaurant or hotel? Did you set up for large-scale banquets or receptions?

Name drop: If you have studied or worked under a famous chef or at a renowned restaurant, hotel, or resort — be sure to mention it prominently, and detail any training or apprenticeship programs that were involved.

Administrative functions: Detail out any responsibilities you had, such as purchasing, inventory control, food and labor cost controls, sales, customer service, or facilities maintenance.

Keywords and phrases:

Amenities	Back-of-the-house operations
Banquet operations	Budget administration
Catering services	Club management
Conference and meeting planning	Corporate Dining Room operations
Corporate service management	Customer retention
Food and Beverage operations	Food cost controls
Front-of-the-house operations	Guest service and satisfaction
Hospitality management	Housekeeping operations
Inventory planning and control	Labor cost controls
Menu planning and pricing	Multi-unit operations
Occupancy management	Portion control
Property development	Purchasing
Resort management	Revenue planning and reporting
Service management	Signature property
Special events planning	Vendor sourcing
VIP relations	

Sample Cover Letter for a Flight Attendant:

NICOLE ROBERTS

292 Lemon Circle – Orlando, FL 39212

(407) 555-9392 – nroberts@email.com

June 3, 2009

Michael Long
Attendant Supervisor
USA Airline
2091 Airport Road
Orlando, FL 39482

Dear Mr. Long:

With over ten years of experience as a flight attendant, I will bring knowledge as well as an outgoing, energetic personality to USA Airline. As you review my attached résumé, please consider the following highlights:

- Experience in both domestic and overseas travel.

- Up-to-date certifications and trained in CPR.

- Currently licensed as a private pilot.

- Customer satisfaction rating of 96 percent.

I very my enjoy my position at Domestic Airline, but as you know the company is going through layoffs and my future here is uncertain. Your advertisement for experienced flight attendants seemed like the perfect opportunity for a career change to an airline with the highlight quality ratings and customer satisfaction.

I know your corporate culture demands that you look for the personality that your customers have come to expect. I know you will find that in me. I look forward to meeting with you to discuss what I can add to your airline service in greater detail, and will contact you next week to schedule an interview.

Thank you so much for your time and consideration!

Sincerely,

Nicole Roberts

Cover Letter Sample for hostess or chef:

JUSTON ROBINSON
837 Jackson Blvd. – Bridgeport, CT 06672 – (203) 555-2928

October 5, 2009

Ms. Simone Livingston
Director of Food Services
High End Resorts, Inc.
3928 Madison Ave.
New York, NY 10983

Dear Ms. Livingston:

I am enclosing a copy of my résumé for your review with the goal of tempting you into considering me as your new head chef of Five Star Dining, due to open in December. I heard about the opening of your new restaurant through Jane Bradley, the manager at my current restaurant, where I work as assistant head chef. I believe you worked with Jane years ago in California.

She mentioned that you have a taste for decadent meals and desserts, and she believes my style of food preparation would be exactly to your liking. I hope to meet with you next week when I will be in New York and perhaps prepare a meal for you.

Until then, I would like to provide you with a brief synopsis of my career accomplishments:

- Created distinctive dishes named after famous guests that frequent our restaurant.

- *Oversaw the preparation of banquette and event foods including wedding cakes, hors d'oeuvres, pates, and main dishes.*

- *Won eight gold medals and two silver in ten years of competition in various culinary competitions.*

- *Featured as "Chef of the Month" in Fine Dining Monthly in March of this year.*

Based on my background and skills, I am confident I can handle the responsibilities of head chef at your new restaurant. I will call you in a couple of days to see if we can schedule a time to meet next week and for you to tell me about your favorite types of food.

Regards,

Juston Robinson

Sample Cover Letter for Hotel Management:

Rajiv Patel

282 East Ave.
Georgetown IL 28272
(278) 555 – 29287
rpatel@email.com

July 23, 2009

Maggie Smith
Smith-Brown Enterprises
Msmith@email.com

Dear Ms. Smith:

If you are in need of a highly qualified Hotel Management Professional, then we have good reason to meet. After researching your firm and your needs, I believe my skill and experience will be of value to your team.

I offer 17 years of successful experience in the hospitality industry at various hotels, serving in positions at the corporate and hotel level. I offer broad-based skills as a controller and hotel accountant that include budgeting, forecasting, auditing, account management, financial statements, accounts payable, accounts receivable, taxes, general ledger, cash flow, profit and loss, and asset management. Throughout my career, I have been recognized as a top performer for consistently meeting and exceeding company goals.

With an eye for detail and excellent organization skills, I meet deadlines and handle multiple projects effortlessly. As a communicator, I am experienced at training and motivating teams of professionals to meet goals and challenges. My dedication to high-quality work is seen in the awards my staff has earned under my leadership.

I feel confident that I can make an immediate positive contribution to your organization. If it appears that my qualifications meet your current needs, I would like to discuss an opportunity to join your team in greater detail in an interview. I look forward to your reply.

Sincerely,

Rajiv Patel

Enclosure: Résumé

Human Resources and Training Careers

Specify experience: Mention the different aspects of human resource management with which you are proficient, like benefits administration, recruiting, payroll, employee relations, and training.

Employee satisfaction: Mention specific ways you have improved the quality of employee performance and job satisfaction. This may include professional development or introducing incentive programs to reward peak performance.

Instructional experience: Mention any experience you have in needs assessment, curriculum planning, course design, online instruction, classroom training, and the design of instruction material.

Keywords and phrases:

American with Disabilities Act (ADA)	Benefits administration
Career paths	Change management
Claims administration	College recruitment
Compensation	Competency-based performance
Corporate cultural communications	Diversity management
Employee communications and relations	Employee empowerment
Employee retention	Employee surveys
Equal employment opportunity (EEO)	Expatriate employment
Grievance proceedings	Human resources (HR)

International employment	Job task analysis
Labor arbitration, negotiations and relations	Leadership development and assessment
Management training and development	Manpower planning
Merit promotion	Multimedia training
Multinational workforce	Organization design and development
Organization needs assessment	Participative management
Performance appraisals and incentives	Performance reengineering
Position classification	Professional recruitment
Regulatory affairs	Retention
Safety training	Self-directed work teams
Staffing	Succession planning
Training and development	Union negotiations and regulation
Wage and salary administration	Workforce reengineering

Cover Letter Sample for a Director of Human Resources:

Alexander Matthews, SPHR

783 West Main Street Apt 134 – West Town, NC 82724
(463) 555 – 9282

Feb. 23, 2008

Daniel Chamberlain

Toys Warehouse

dchamberlain@email.com

Dear Mr. Chamberlain:

*Your recent advertisement on website.com for a **Director of Human Resources** captured my interest because your needs and my background are a close match.*

As a Human Resource Director with more than 20 years of experience, I am known for my creativity, my customer-service record, and my focus on bottom-line results. My career accomplishments include successfully re-engineering departments to make them more streamlined and in touch with today's technologies, as well as corporate recruiting, staffing, and employee development programs.

Please note that while directing the overall human resource department, I also remain up-to-date in all core HR functions, including new state regulations and procedures to ensure that all paperwork is being filled out and properly filed.

My major projects have included benefits/compensation design, HRIS selection and implementation, and large-scale recruitment activities in business pre-opening situations (over 2,500 employees recruited).

I would welcome the opportunity to speak with you more in depth about your needs and how I can contribute immediately to your success. I will follow up in the next few days to ensure that you received my materials and answer any preliminary questions you may have.

Best regards,

Alexander Matthews

Enclosure: Résumé

Sample Cover Letter for a Recruiter:

KATLYNN SMITH
32 Frosty Way — City, State 49292
(483) 555-9392 — Katlynns@email.com

Dec. 31, 2009

Carol Williams
Hiring Manager
Southwest Recruiting, Inc.
382 East Line Ave.
City, State 41361

Dear Ms. Williams:

*It is with great enthusiasm that I am submitting my résumé for consideration as a **recruiter** within your organization. The strong people and communication skills I mastered in several customer-centered environments make me an ideal candidate to access, evaluate, and place the right people in the right positions. As you review my attached résumé, please consider the following highlights:*

- *Possess a strong work ethic and exceptional team skills.*

- *Proven experience in customer service positions, including customer relations, cash handling, and point of sale operation.*

- *Ability to close major sale opportunities due to strong relationship building and presentation skills.*

- *Significant experience operating cash registers and other computerized equipment within stores.*

- *Excellent communication and interpersonal skills; takes initiative in managing and developing effective working relationships with clients.*

- *Ability to adapt quickly in new and changing business, social, and cultural environments.*

My record of schoolwork, employment, and volunteer activities demonstrates attributes that make me a valuable employee. In all of my employment and volunteer positions, I have maintained an excellent record of being on time, prepared, and eager to take on new responsibilities.

Thank you for your time and consideration. I look forward to scheduling a personal interview with you and will contact your office later in the week to do so at your convenience. I look forward to speaking with you soon.

Sincerely,

Katlynn Smith

Sample Cover Letter:

JULIA WALLACE

1401 East Harbor Road – Bridgetown, NH 10392

(341) 555-9283 – juleswallace@email.com

November 5, 2008

ABC Corp
Attn: Senior Manager, International Training
1234 Main Street
Bridgetown, NH 10558

Dear Mr. Jones:

I am writing to express my interest in the **senior manager of international training** position with your company. I'm excited about joining a company that has been founded on a premise of being "not only a company, but a community based on support, trust, and independence through interdependence."

With ten years of training experience, seven years of management and leadership experience, and 20 years of partnering and communicating with team members, customers, corporate executives, and various governmental organizations, I truly believe I can assist in helping franchisees and ABC Corp in continuing success.

As a training specialist and program coordinator with the state of Iowa, I was responsible for developing and delivering training for 300 plus staff, determining the best training methodology, and leading a team of five trainers to successfully deliver quality training. As the Training Center Manager for VITREX Corporation, I led a team of six trainers, helping them develop their skills in delivering quality training for authorized Microsoft and Novell training classes.

My self-initiative and desire to help others succeed along with me will be a wonderful asset to ABC Corp.'s training program. The attached résumé highlights my background and qualifications. I am thrilled about this opportunity and welcome the chance to provide specific examples of my ten years of training experience.

Thank you for your time and consideration. Please do not hesitate to contact me if you have any questions. I look forward to hearing from you.

Sincerely,

Julia Wallace

(This letter was prepared by contributor Sonya Dutcher)

Sample Cover Letter

MARIA BARKER
10038 Gold Gate Drive – Chicago, IL 66830
(717) 555- 8728 – mbarker@email.com

January 13, 2009

Jim Fisher
Hiring Manager -XYZ Software
jimfisher@email.com
RE: Worldwide Technical Training Director
Job Code: 6087

Dear Mr. Fisher:

*I am writing to apply for the **worldwide technical training director** position responsible for planning, organizing, and directing all technical training provided to internal and external XYZ customers worldwide.*

With over ten years training and seven years management experience, I believe I can ensure that the XYZ support technicians, presales, professional services, and selected partners receive timely and accurate new hire training, new product training, and continuing educations on existing products.

My interest in this position goes beyond the fact that this is an excellent and solid career move. Throughout my professional career, I have had two primary focal areas – leadership and training. This focus has been driven by my passion to help people learn and succeed in their professional careers and personal development.

During my career path, I have had the chance to participate with many levels of management and staff, manage projects and personnel, oversee budget expenditures, prove my ability to grasp technical system concepts, and achieve short/long-term goals.

As a current XYZ Software employee in a transitional position scheduled to end June 2009, I have to say, I would appreciate the opportunity to continue with a company that is passionate about providing innovative products and deep IT experience to customers with a continued focus on what those customers need most.

Attached is my résumé, which exemplifies my experience to date. I am looking forward to having a more detailed discussion about my qualifications and how they can bring value to XYZ Software's internal and external customers.

Sincerely,

Maria Barker

(This letter was prepared by contributor Sonya Dutcher and was written in Arial at font size 10.5)

Sample Cover Letter for a Corporate Trainer:

Michaela Scott

3000 Mountain View Lane – Boulder, CO 98372 – (892) 555-8392 – mcscott79@email.com

Jan 15, 2009

Mr. Timothy Logan
Human Resource Manager
298 Archer Blvd.
Boulder, CO 92827

Dear Mr. Logan:

My career includes more than eight years of experience in training, marketing, and customer service. My attached résumé details how my skill sets match up ideally with the requirements you listed in your job posting on website.com for an assistant manager of corporate training. Please allow me to draw your attention to a few specific highlights from my career.

- ***Program Development**: I designed and delivered training material for technical and business skill development including a creative (and successful) plan to increase training opportunities for customer service reps in a call center environment, without taking away from their phone time.*

- ***Skill Assessment**: I proposed and facilitated peer feedback session in which employees with varying strengths were grouped so that participants would benefit by learning from each other.*

- ***Coaching Techniques**: I co-designed a thriving in-house model for coaching customer service representatives on the results of their monitoring. I created a related training module, tested, and then employed it in actual coaching sessions.*

I am confident in my ability to make a similar positive contribution to your company immediately upon hire. I welcome the opportunity to interview with you and look forward to hearing from you soon to schedule an interview.

Respectfully,

Michaela Scott

(This letter was written in Tahoma in font size 10).

Law Enforcement and Legal Careers

Credentials: In this profession, credentials and certifications are paramount. Prominently mention firearms training, special tactics, or special investigative credentials. For attorneys, list the courts and state in which you are admitted to practice.

Measures of performance: Be specific in this regard. As an attorney, how many cases have you tried at what level of court? How many cases have you won? What is your success rate at closing cases? How have you contributed toward the conviction rate or crime rate reduction? As a police officer, how many arrests have you made?

Administrative experience: Make mention of any experience in personnel training, supervision, record-keeping, report preparation, regulatory review, and compliance.

Keywords and phrases for **Lawyers**:

Acquisition	Adjudication
Antitrust	Briefs
Client management	Competitive intelligence
Corporate bylaws	Cross-border transactions
Depositions	Discovery
Due diligence	Ethics
Fraud	General and limited partnership
Intellectual property	Interrogatory
Joint venture	Judicial affairs
Juris Doctor (JD)	Landmark decision
Legal advocacy	Legal research
Legislative review and analysis	Licensing

Limited liability corporation (LLC)	Litigation
Mediation	Memoranda
Mergers	Motions
Negotiations	Personal injury
Risk management	SEC affairs
Settlement negotiations	Shareholder relations
Signature authority	Technology transfer
Trade secrets	Trademark
Types of law: administrative, case, contracts, copyright, corporate, criminal, employment, environmental, family, labor, patent, personal injury, probate, real estate, tax, transactions, trial and workers' compensation.	Unfair competition

Keywords and phrases for **Law Enforcement**:

Arrests and prosecution	Asset protection
Case closure rate	Community outreach
Corporate fraud	Corporate security
Courtroom proceedings	Criminal investigations
Crisis communication & response	Electronic surveillance
Emergency planning & response	Emergency preparedness
Industrial espionage	Industrial security
Interrogation	Investigations management
Law enforcement	Media and public relations
Personal protection	Safety training
Search and seizure	Security operations
Surveillance	Tactical field operations
VIP protections	White-collar crime

Cover Letter for an Attorney in response to an advertisement:

KEVIN T. TOWNSON
7894 Washington Ave.
Columbia, MD. 21049
(410) 555-8739

May 15, 2009

Mr. Phillip E. Smith
Manager of Administrative Employment
Specialty Labs
899 Third Street
Baltimore, MD 28398

Dear Mr. Smith:

*While browsing the current issue of Legal Briefs, I noticed your advertisement for a **patent attorney**. I interned for a pharmaceutical company while obtaining my B.S. in chemistry and continue to take great interest in the industry today. My attached résumé will demonstrate my knowledge of your industry and my experience as a patent attorney.*

I meet your specified requirements in the following ways:

- *I graduated magnum cum laude in my undergraduate degree from the University of Virginia. My legal degree is from Georgetown University.*

- *I currently work for Widget, USA — a small part manufacturing company — as their principal attorney in the patent area.*

- *In my five years of employment, I wrote over 50 patent applications for parts they developed — 30 of which were approved.*

- *During that same time, I successfully defended their patents in court ten times.*

I followed the Stephan Smith case that your company lost last September and gave serious consideration to what I would have done differently. I would like to share my thoughts with you on that subject as a demonstration of how my skills will meet your need for a creative, talented patent attorney. I look forward to scheduling a meeting with you at your earliest convenience.

Best regards,

Kevin Townson

Sample "Broadcast" Letter for a Lawyer/Law Student:

AMANDA VAN HORN

555 E. Byron Place, Apt. 2 - King of Prussia, PA 19406

(856)-555-6316 - avanhorn@email.com

May 14, 2009

Robert Jones
Jones Law Firm
rjones@email.com

Dear Mr. Jones:

It is with genuine enthusiasm and interest that I offer my résumé for your review and offer a brief summary of how my skills may benefit the efforts of your law firm. I am confident that my background and education have more than adequately prepared me and provided me the necessary skills to perform competently and efficiently as an attorney with your firm.

I am a 2009 LL.M. (Taxation) candidate at Villanova University School of Law and I will graduate in less than one week. My graduate tax education at Villanova University has given me extensive knowledge of nearly all aspects of taxation, including estate planning, taxation of trusts and estates, drafting of estate planning documents, taxation of corporations and partnerships, property dispositions, and tax research and writing.

My time in the graduate tax program at Villanova University has also helped me to strengthen the verbal and written communication skills and analytical problem solving skills I first honed at Roger Williams University School of Law, from which I graduated in 2007. In that same year, I also sat for and passed both the Pennsylvania and New Jersey Bar Examinations.

Prior to law school, I attended Drury University, where I graduated magna cum laude with a double major in both mathematics and criminology, and a minor in global studies. My criminology major helped me first gain appreciation for the law and legal studies, and presented me with the opportunity to complete a semester-long internship as a clerk for the Greene County, Missouri Drug Court.

For the past two years, I volunteered my time to VITA (Volunteer Income Tax Assistance), where I have prepared tax returns for middle-to-low income individuals who could neither prepare them on their own nor afford to pay for preparation.

My academic record and background, coupled with my passion for law and estate planning, make me an ideal candidate. I would greatly appreciate the opportunity to meet with you to discuss my qualifications in further detail. I look forward to hearing from you. Thank you very much for your time and consideration.

Sincerely,

Amanda Van Horn

(This cover letter was prepared by contributor Amy Van Fossen and was written in Arial at font size 10)

Sample Referral Cover Letter for an Attorney:

JANICE WILLIAMS
121 East Bird Blvd.
Small Town WI 84932
(978) 555-8373
Jwilliams41868@email.com

September 7, 2009

Ms. Marsha Long
Vice President & General Counsel
Bradley, White and Jones
4783 Lincoln Ave.
Big Town WI 83272

Dear Ms. Long:

Ashley Grant, one of my colleagues at Swanson Inc., suggested that I contact you. I understand that you and Ashley began your careers together at Cheese America and worked together for over ten years. She speaks very highly of you.

Ms. Long, I am a corporate attorney and have worked in the legal division of Swanson Inc., for three years since my graduation from Yale Law School in 2006. My area of concentration has been Human Resource law, although I assisted colleagues in both patent and anti-trust cases.

I have attached a copy of my résumé for your reference.

My husband, Jack, and I have decided to relocate to Big Town. Jack has been offered a wonderful career opportunity there that we feel would be a mistake for him to turn down. Therefore, I find myself searching for a position that will be a positive career move for me as well. Ashley was confident you would be able to assist me in my search.

Even if you do not know of any specific openings for someone with my credentials, I would like to meet with you when I am in town the first week of October. Ashley thought you might be able to introduce me to some of your colleagues as well to give me a jumpstart on my networking goals in your community. Thank you for your assistance in this matter.

Sincerely,

Janice Williams

Sample Cover Letter for Chief of Police:

Nigel Cunningham
291 Washington Ave. — Mid Town, State 92020
Home: (928) 555-9292 — Cell: (938) 555-3922

City of Sister Town
Attn: Sara Walsh
Head of Human Resources
932 Line Street Suite 2
Sister Town, State 93022

Dear Ms. Walsh:

In response to your search for a chief of police, I bring over 20 years of experience that showcases leadership, commitment to justice, successful case closure rates, and a desire to ensure a safe environment for Sister Town's citizens to enjoy.

I grew up in Sister Town and still have strong ties to the community. My oldest son is getting ready to start high school and I would love for him to attend Sister Town High. Moving back to Sister Town and serving its people as Chief of Police would be the perfect career move for me at this time. In return, I would give Sister Town the heart-felt dedication she deserves to clean streets, lower crime rates, and education programs.

My career in law enforcement began as a beat cop in Sister Town. Several years later, I moved with my wife to Mid Town and accepted a promotion to Detective. I currently serve as my department's Lieutenant and am therefore completely versed in the administrative side of law that the Chief position would require.

Under my leadership, my department's case closure rate increased to 90 percent and each officer volunteers one weekend a month a community education function such as proper use of child seats, gun cleaning safety, or instructing CPR courses. I will inspire that same commitment to justice and the community from my police force as Chief in Sister Town.

After you review my attached résumé, I would enjoy meeting with the search committee to discuss my qualifications in greater detail. I look forward to hearing from you in that regards. Thank you for your consideration.

Respectfully,

Nigel Cunningham

Manufacturing and Operations Careers

Training: Highlight your experience and training in principles and methods such as Lean Manufacturing, Six Sigma, and ISO standards.

Dollar figures: Include information about your contributions to process improvements, scrap reduction, and other innovations that reduce production costs. When possible, discuss the value or percentage of money saved by your efforts.

Production: Discuss the various operations and processes you have experience with such as cell manufacturing, assembly line, and fabrication. Also discuss your ability to meet deadlines and the quality of product you produce. Back your statements up with numbers or percentages whenever possible.

Keywords and phrases:

Asset management	Automated manufacturing
Best-in-class	Capacity planning
Capital project & budget	Cell manufacturing
Computer integrated manufacturing (CIM)	Concurrent engineering
Continues improvement	Cost reductions & avoidance
Cross-functional teams	Cycle time reduction
Distribution management	Efficiency improvement
Environmental health & safety	Equipment management
Ergonomically efficient	Inventory control
Labor relations & efficiency	Logistics management
Manufacturing engineering & integration	Manufacturing technology
Master schedule	Multi-site operations
OSHA — operational safety & health administration	On-time delivery
Operating budget	Operations management
Optimization	Order fulfillment & processing
Outsourcing	Performance improvement
Physical inventory	Pilot management
Plant operations	Process automation
Process redesign/reengineering	Product development & engineering
Production forecasting	Production management
Productivity improvement	Profit & loss management
Project budget	Purchasing management
Quality control & quality assurance	Regulatory compliance
Safety training & management	Shipping & receiving operations

Spares & repairs management	Technology integration
Union negotiations	Vendor management
Warehousing operations	Workforce management

Sample Cover Letter for Director of Operations:

ERIN McCORMICK   emccormick@email.com
298 South Bend Ave.   Home: (283) 555-9282
Jackson, Mississippi 49383   Cell: (283) 555-3822

April 13, 2009

Paul Williams
Manufacturing Recruiters
2999 Roundabout Way
Jackson, Mississippi 29384

Dear Mr. Williams:

Building organizational value and profitability while maintaining a high standard of customer service is my expertise. Throughout my tenure with Gulf Coast Manufacturing, currently as the National Director of Operations, my teams pioneered innovative solutions to improve installation cycle times, reduce operating costs, enhance customer satisfaction, and accelerate top-line revenue.

With more than 17 years of leadership detailed in my enclosed résumé, I offer a strong track record highlighted by:

- *Strategic vision and leadership of a manufacturing division that grew from $398 million to $500 million in less than four years with a 45 percent cycle time reduction, a 60 percent improvement in forecasting, and a five-point increase in our customer satisfaction index.*

- Training, development, and leadership of high-performance, multi-discipline professionals in production operations, Logistics and supply, engineering project management, and installation service.

- Profit and Loss accountability for multi-million dollar operations ranging from $5 million to $500 million with teams sized from 15-450.

With a demonstrated ability to produce positive change and strengthen a company, my goal is another senior-level position with an organization in need of a strong, decisive leader. I am anticipating a six-figure package and will consider relocating, since you recruit throughout the Gulf Coast. Thank you for your time and consideration. I look forward to meeting with you to discuss specific opportunities with your client companies.

Regards,

Erin McCormick

Sample "cold-call" letter for parts manufacturer:

Harold "Harry" Williams   hwilliams86@email.com
7849 North Center Street   Residence: (489) 555-9899
West Bend, WI 58939   Mobile: (478) 555-9878

June 5, 2009

Ms. Susan Henderson
Parts and Supplies
78476 Parts Drive
Nonamesville, CA 97680

Dear Ms. Henderson:

I consider myself extremely fortunate to have come across an article in The Techno Gadget Gazette that states you will soon be expanding into West Bend. I have often found myself admiring the quality of your inventions and long for the opportunity to join a company who strives to be a driving force in the techno gadget industry.

I just recently graduated from West State University with a major in technological design and manufacturing. I specialized in parts and design. I know that your company has maintained a 57 percent market share for close to a decade now, gaining new patents yearly while providing gadgetry to both domestic and international consumers. I studied your breakthroughs in artificial intelligence with great admiration.

I know that being a recent graduate, I may lack the experience you seek, but my participation in a number of studies involving artificial intelligence may impress you. Most notably, I was a research assistant for Frank Smith on his experimental design for automated kitchen devices, which received many exceptional reviews last summer and is pending patent now.

After you review my attached résumé, I hope you take an interest in me for your new West Bend office. I look forward to hearing from you soon.

Regards,

Harold Williams

Sample Cover Letter for Sawmill Manager:

Jeffery VanBuren
2482 Lakeview Blvd. — Leesburg, Wyoming 84732
(382) 555-3938 — jvanburen@email.com

March 3, 2009

Mr. Charles Jackson
Foresting Inc.
charlesjackson@email.com

Dear Mr. Jackson:

With over 21 years of experience in the sawmill industry, I am ideally suited to meet your needs for a **sawmill manager**. I have progressively handled roles with greater responsibility and managerial demands. I began work in my father's sawmill and stayed in the industry after he died and we were forced to sell his business to a larger corporation.

As my résumé will show, my lengthy experience as a sawmill worker, supervisor, manager, and superintendent make me the ideal candidate for this position. Please allow me to draw your attention to a few highlights of my career:

- A focus on health and safety: This is my proudest achievement. Through my initiatives as the safety prevention officer for my current employer, I turned around what was once a terrible safety record to one that exceeds all health codes and regulations.

- Experience in mill planning and upgrading: Over the years, I led several projects to plan new mills or expand existing *ones. In fact, I was part of the team that expanded my father's old mill when it was bought out 19 years ago.*

- *Instructional experience: Shortly into my career, I found myself in a training role for new employees. I have found this to be one of my great talents, as I enjoy teaching people to master the trade I love.*

- *Administrative experience: The last eight years of my career have led me to gain an increasing amount of experience with employee and customer relations, including contract writing, payroll preparations, and employee evaluations.*

Thank you for reviewing my résumé. I look forward to sharing with you my thoughts about how I could make an immediate positive impact as your sawmill manager.

Regards,

Jeffery VanBuren

Sample Referral Letter for an Operations Manager:

JACK CASSELLA
24 High Street — Eustis, FL 34929
(352) 555-9392 — jcassella@email.com

August 15, 2009

Tim Rice
Recruiter
Corporate Recruiting, Inc.
81559 State St.
Sanford, FL 31361

Dear Mr. Rice:

At the Medical Device Workshop last month in Tampa, I ran into Shay Matthews while viewing a presentation on the nursing home equipment you are introducing this winter. After the presentation, I mentioned to her that I was looking for a new employment opportunity and she suggested I get in touch with you.

She mentioned that you are currently building a Medical Device Manufacturing facility in Miami and that you are recruiting for the position of operations manager. With nearly nine years of experience in that position, I have the right balance of skills and abilities necessary for a successful start-up plant.

I first worked with Shay after I graduated from Southern Georgia University with my degree in management. As you know, she was working for a headhunting firm in Georgia at that time, and she placed me with Harrison Operations at their Atlanta plant where I worked for five years as the assistant operations manager. By contributing to their 30 percent increase in productivity during those years, I was promoted to their Florida branch when they opened it eight years ago. Since then, my team received top recognition for safety, satisfaction, efficiency, and productivity. I am a proven leader with an employee satisfaction rating of 95 percent for the third year in a row.

Shay mentioned that you will actively start looking to fill this position by fourth quarter. I realize you may need to conduct an extensive search, but I would like to meet with you to discuss how I can best contribute to your company in this role. I will call you at your office next week to schedule an interview.

Respectfully,

Jack Cassella

Enclosure: Résumé

Photography, Graphic Design, and Artistic Careers

Portfolio: Have examples of your work to showcase for any potential employer. Be it an online portfolio or a physical one — you need to show off your capability with real life examples of your work.

Technological knowledge: Your specialty might be creativity, but we operate in a digital, computer generated world. Talk about all the computer programs and other hardware in which you are trained and proficient.

People skills: Since you often work with people as the subject of your work, include details about your customer service and people skills.

Aperture settings	Black and white
Cameras	Digital Single Lens Reflex (DSLR)
Film	F-stop
Graphic design	Illustration
JPEG	Landscape
Layout	Logos
Macro	Model
Photojournalism	Photoshop
Photo manipulation	Photo restoration
Portfolio	Portrait
Post Processing	Sports
Video editing	Web graphics
Wedding	

Cover Letter Sample for a Photographer:

Zoey Matthews
2323 Torn Street
Star City NY, 87363
(201) 555 - 3726

Feb. 23, 2009

Dear Ms. Jones:

*Capturing the perfect smile of a beautiful baby — nothing could be more rewarding than that, or more challenging. But I excel at capturing difficult images, and I would like to bring that talent to your staff if you will consider me for the **staff photographer** position you have available. I have attached my résumé and the requested samples of my work.*

In my four years as a professional photographer, I have acquired a vast amount of experience and knowledge. This is due mostly to my time spent as a field assistant to Sam Waters — the well — known sports photographer for the Washington Post.

After leaving his employment, I moved to New York with a friend as we decided to live our dreams in the Big Apple. I realize I should be jaded by now, but perhaps since I grew up in a large metropolitan area, I was well-prepared for what New York City would be like. I love the energy and vibe of this city. I currently work as a portrait photographer at Beautiful Smiles Studios.

I love my current position, but I read in your advertisement that you not only do portraits but weddings, company events, and even landscape photography. With the training you provide and my natural talent at capturing the perfect shot, I will become one of your best photographers within months.

I am willing to start at the very basic level and will be more than happy to help set up for shoots on different locations, or to maintain the studio, and would even enjoy learning more about the lab side of things in terms of developing the pictures.

Thank you very much for taking the time to read this letter. I hope that I have piqued your interest with my enthusiasm. After you have reviewed my enclosed submissions, I hope you will decide to schedule an interview with me. I look forward to hearing from you soon.

Sincerely,

Zoey Matthews

Sample Cover Letter for a Student graduating looking for a Graphic Design job:

MICHELLE THOMAS
73 Main Street
City, State 29382
(123)-555-7890

April 10, 2009

Ms. Daniela Bergess
Major Corporation
Street
New York, NY 12345

Dear Ms. Bergess:

In May of this year, I will receive my B.A. degree in fine arts with a major in graphic design. Since I am interested in Major Corporation, I am writing you to inquire about entry-level career op-

portunities which may exist in your design or advertising departments.

With experience in designing various kinds of products, including industrial products and packing material, I believe my talents will serve your company well. My enclosed résumé details my education, interests, and work experience. Additionally, I have included samples of freelance work done while completing my studies.

My interest in Major Corporation comes from your outstanding reputation, both for your customer service and your high-quality products. I feel my qualifications are competitive and I would an asset to your company. It would be a joy to contribute to the company's continued success.

After you have had an opportunity to review my résumé and sample work, I would like to meet with you at your earliest convenience since I believe a personal interview is the best way to determine if I am the perfect fit for your organization. Thank you for your consideration. I look forward to meeting with you soon.

Sincerely,

Michelle Thomas

(This cover letter was written in Times New Roman in font size 12).

Cover Letter Sample for a Graphic Designer:

Richard Jones
4120 SW 45th Street
Orlando, Florida 34455
(407)-555-0559 (H) / (407)-555-7870 (C)
richardjones400@email.com

February 16, 2009

Mr. Daniel Brown
Southeast Publishing Group, Inc.
15 SW 8th Ave
Orlando, Florida 36655

Dear Mr. Brown,

I would like to express my interest in the **graphic artist/ designer** position that is available at Southeast Publishing. I am well trained in the areas of graphic design and video production, and I am excited about the opportunity to work for such a diverse corporation.

For the last nine years, I have been privileged to serve at Nightingale Church as the director of media. I was responsible for managing the Television, Graphics, and Advertising departments. In my time there, I transformed their media department from a single computer and page layout program to a state-of-the-art department with new computer equipment, design software, and video equipment. With these tools, we produce professional grade graphics for many different venues at the church, including books, brochures, banners, newspapers, and magazines. This actually saves the church thousands of dollars every year by producing material in house that they would have to otherwise outsource.

Once you review my résumé, I believe you will agree with me that my experience appears to be an ideal match for your opening. I look forward to speaking with you about a possible fit into your organization. Thank you for your time and consideration, and I hope to be hearing from you soon.

Sincerely,

Richard Jones

(This cover letter was written in Arial at font size 12)

Sample Cover Letter for Glassblower/Jewelry Designer:

ANGELA KRECK
1593 Forest Circle — City, State 49920
(382) 555-2929 — akreck@email.com

March 3, 2009

Trish Wallace
General Manager
Women's Jewelry Boutique
291 Main Street
City, State 49292

Dear Ms. Wallace:

After visiting your lovely store last month, I could not stop thinking about how the jewelry I design with my husband would look in your store. Then I saw your advertisement for a freelance jewelry designer in the Daily Gazette and I knew I had to send you samples of my work in hopes you agree with me that my style matches yours perfectly.

I have enclosed my résumé and work samples for you to review. While the appearance of my samples will have to speak for themselves, I would like to highlight a few things from my career that should speak on the quality of the product I produce:

- *A year apprenticeship with a journeyman glassblower and his wife who designs jewelry from his work.*

- *Certification in gemology.*

- *Certification to work with fine gems such as diamonds, emeralds, and rubies.*

- *Customer satisfaction ratings of 90 percent.*

If after reviewing my submissions you would like to speak with me further, I would greatly enjoy meeting with you. Thank you for your consideration.

Sincerely,

Angela

Sales, Marketing, and Customer Service Careers

Statistics: Use figures to quantify your achievements whenever possible. Show percentage increases in revenue, your ranking among associates, or the number of new accounts your closed.

Necessary skills: Highlight your consultative, selling, and relationship-building skills. Show your ability to connect to customers, assess their needs, and recommend the right solutions.

Show diversity: Mention the various product categories for which you possess knowledge or the types of customers you are trained to serve (business-to-business or business-to-consumer, for example).

Keywords and phrases:

Account development & management	Account retention
Brand management	Campaign management
Competitive analysis	Customer communications
Customer development & retention	Customer focus groups & surveys
Customer loyalty	Customer management
Customer needs assessment	Customer service & satisfaction
Direct-mail & direct-response marketing	Direct and indirect sales
Distribution manager	E-business and E-commerce
Emerging markets	Field sales management
Field service operations	Global markets & sales
Headquarters account management	High-impact presentations
Incentive planning	Inbound service operations
International sales & trade	Key account management
Margin improvement	Market launch
Market positioning	Market research & surveys
Market-share ratings	Marketing strategy
Multichannel distribution & sales	Multimedia advertising & communications
National account management	Negotiations
New market development	Order processing & fulfillment
Outbound service operations	Process simplification
Product development, launch & introduction	Product life-cycle management
Product line rationalization	Product positioning
Profit & loss management	Profit growth
Promotions	Public relations & speaking
Records management	Relationship management
Revenue stream and growth	Sales forecasting

Sales presentation and closing	Sales training
Service benchmarks & measures	Service delivery
Service quality	Telemarketing & telesales operations
Team building/leadership	Trend analysis

Sample Cover letter for Sales:

BRIDGET JONES

1234 Main Street w Phoenix, AZ 85016

bridgetjones@email.com – w (602) 555-0123

February 11, 2009

David Jones
Vice President of Sales
ABC Company
12345 Cactus Road
Scottsdale, AZ 85260

Dear Mr. Jones:

I am writing this letter in response to your current opening for a regional sales account manager. I am very interested in building a career with ABC Company due to your award-winning solutions, strong partnerships, and prestigious customer base, and would love to have the opportunity to play a part in the company's continued success in 2009.

I am confident I would be a great asset to your organization and would make a valuable contribution, due in part to my following achievements:

- *Experience — Proven software sales executive with over five years of industry experience, selling identity and access management, auditing, and security solutions.*

- *Drive and Ambition — Acknowledged for proven success in various "hunter" and customer-facing sales positions due to an outstanding work ethic, as well as IT problem-solving and persuasive communication skills.*

- *Education — Degree in business administration, University of Arizona.*

As an accomplished solution sales professional, I feel I can add immediate value to the ABC Company team and be an immediate contributor, in large part due to my current software sales experience in both mid-market and enterprise roles, as well as my contagious energy and strong drive for success. I would highly value the opportunity to work for the market leader.

Enclosed you'll find my résumé further detailing my career accomplishments. I would welcome the opportunity to meet with you to discuss my qualifications, and I look forward to hearing from you.

Best Regards,

Bridget Jones

(This letter was prepared by contributor Allison Shvets and was written in Arial at font size 10)

Sample Cover Letter for Sales Director:

Amber Smith
837 Mill Street – Colorado City, Colorado 98372
(827) 555- 2928 - asmith@email.com

Feb. 24, 2009

Mr. Rob Patterson
Sales R Us
rpatterson@email.com

Dear Mr. Patterson:

Sales and marketing is about developing and implementing an innovative and tactical vision that will generate outstanding results and profitability. My leadership abilities and extensive hands-on experience will benefit you as your **sales director** *because I will produce a vision that inspires your staff to not only meet, but exceed your expectations. I have attached my résumé for your consideration.*

Promoted to increasingly challenging and responsible positions, I have mastered the following skills in my 19 years of experience:

- **Leadership***: With an excellent record in recruitment, motivation, and performance of sales team, I currently manage a team of nine that has exceeded their margin target by 10-30 percent each fiscal quarter for three years.*

- **Business development***: I demonstrated the ability to asses a marketplace and uncover new clients in my current and last position, increasing clientele for both business by 25 percent over five years.*

- **Relationship management***: I possess solid skills in forging and solidifying client, partner, and vendor relationships. This is demonstrated by my proven negotiating skills in writing over 30 new contracts per year for the last five years.*

*My skills at leading sales teams to conceptualize, build, and imple-
ment ground-breaking marketing strategies will bring Sales R Us
from the number four slot to the number one slot in the industry in
six months. I am excited by the opportunity to meet with you and
will contact you shortly to schedule an interview at your earliest
convenience.*

Best regards,

Amber Smith

Sample Cover Letter For Customer Service Representative:

LISA KARP
2728 Charmed Street
San Francisco, CA, 92807
(563) 555-8858
lisakarp@email.com

March 7, 2009

Prudence Halliwell
USA Annuity and Life Insurance Company
555 Locust Street
San Francisco, CA 99999

Dear Ms. Halliwell:

*It is twice as hard to attract a new customer as it is to retain a
current one. USA is one of the few companies that understand
this fact, and demonstrates this maxim by its willingness to put
customer satisfaction first. That is why I am excited to apply for
the position of* **customer contact center representative** *within
your organization. With over five years of experience in customer
satisfaction, I am a perfect match for USA.*

During my previous employment at a market research firm, I conducted phone surveys on consumer products. I was consistently commended by my superiors and those I spoke with on the phone for my friendly tone and demeanor and my ability to make a long, tedious process of a phone survey more enjoyable. Through the combination of skills I gained during my previous jobs, I developed the ability to interact with a wide variety of people. I assessed their needs and communicated with them in a pleasant and effective manner, ensuring customer satisfaction.

As a recent Master's graduate, I bring education and experience to this position that are detailed in my attached résumé. After you review it, I would appreciate meeting with you to further discuss the immediate positive impact I can make for your team. Thank you for your time and consideration.

Sincerely,

Lisa Karp

(This cover letter was prepared by contributor Shira Karp)

Sample Cover Letter for a Marketing Manager:

JASON ROBINSON

392 Pine Tree Blvd. – Cincinnati, OH 45983

(513) 555- 9849 – jasonrobertrobinson@email.com

September 22, 2009

Mr. Jerry Vahn
Sports Incorporated
2948 Park Street Suite 5
Cincinnati, OH 45398

Dear Mr. Vahn:

Your advertised position for a marketing manager was like a dream come true for someone who has a passion for sports and marketing like I do. I am forwarding you my résumé, but let me take this opportunity to explain how I can make that dream a reality by highlighting how my background meets the specific requirements you listed:

- *I obtained bachelor's degrees in marketing and finance from Penn State. That education is enhanced with three years of experience in the marketing department with Procter & Gamble.*

- *Education and experience provided me a solid understanding of marketing fundamentals. I work with qualitative and quantitative research methods on a daily basis. I wrote and directed the writing of ad copy for multiple media, managing advertising budgets for up to $3 million dollars.*

- *In high school, I played varsity soccer and baseball. I attended Penn State on an athletic scholarship, where I played baseball for three years until I was in a car accident where I broke my arm. My pitching arm was never the same after that, but my love for sports never waned and I still enjoy running, weightlifting, swimming, snowboarding, and flag football with friends.*

- *I am proficient in Microsoft Word, Excel, and PowerPoint, using each of them in my daily work.*

- *I excel in my current position, which requires solid communication skills, including a talent for public speaking as well as the ability to give clear directions on expectations.*

After you have fully reviewed my résumé, I hope that you will want to schedule me for an interview. I look forward to meeting you at that time. Thank you for your consideration.

Regards,

Jason Robinson

Sample Cover Letter:

KAREN D. BROWN
18 Manchester Lane, Dovenshire NJ 21930

(498) 555-2932
kdb@email.com

October 5, 2009

James Davidson
Sales Director
Higher Marketing Inc.
1837 Market Ave.
Dovenshire NJ 21928

Dear Mr. Davidson:

In today's dynamic global economy, successful business development initiatives are essential to stay ahead of the competition and position your company as a high-tech leader. As an executive with award-winning sales results, proven negotiation skills, and relationship-building expertise, I:

- *Transformed sales focus to next-gen technology business, growing sales 100 percent to $60 million.*

- *Delivered a 350 percent sales increase in management of a national UPS account; attained 125 percent of goal.*

- *Led entry into the untapped international market; created an $8 million pipeline in eight months.*

While my recent experience and contributions have been within a large company environment, I welcome any challenge as a hunter of new business. I invite you to review the enclosed résumé, and then call me to discuss your competitive challenges, the needs of your customers, and the sales solutions I can provide.

Sincerely,

Karen Brown

(This cover letter was prepared by contributor Danny Huffman and was written in Tahoma with font size 11.)

Sample Cover Letter:

Margaret "Peg" Mitchell

393 West 5th Street — Bloomburg, CT 23728 — (284) 555-2929

April 8, 2009

Dear Mr. Jonathan Franklin:

*With documented success forging strategic relationships to maximize revenue growth, I am writing in response to your search for a **senior sales representative**. Skilled in product knowledge, troubleshooting, competitive advantage, construction project management, customer needs, and logistics/procurement/ delivery, I will be a valuable asset within your organization.*

During my 15 plus years of experience, I turned around an under-performing distribution center, enabling the branch to rank within the 15 top branches among 65 locations. In addition, I decreased inventory from $2.9 million to $500,000, increased revenue 300 percent in two years, and drove sales from $200,000 to $2 million in five years. I am confident I will equally impact your company.

Moreover, I maintain in-depth product knowledge to boost overall customer satisfaction and deliver new, repeat, and referral business. Eager to detail my achievements and discuss your strategic plans, I look forward to your reply. Meanwhile, thank you for your attention.

Sincerely,

Peg Mitchell

(This cover letter was prepared by contributor Danny Huffman and was written in Arial with font size 12)

Skilled Trades Careers

Certifications and training: Highlight specific training programs, internships, and apprenticeships you have completed. Also include additional certifications or licenses you hold.

New technology: Highlight your experience with the latest technology — the newest software, programming, or other tools that are new to the industry.

Range: Showcase your range of experience by listing all the skill sets you specialize in.

Leadership: If you are considered a master tradesman and have apprenticed others underneath you, be sure to mention the number of students you have instructed and their success rate.

Keywords and phrases:

Blueprints and drawings	Contract administration
Crew supervision	Customer relations
Electrical, plumbing, & HVAC	Fault Isolation & analysis
Maintenance and repair	Preventative maintenance
Project management	Project scheduling & documentation
Project specifications	Regulatory compliance
Residential & commercial projects	Scope-of-work documents
Testing & troubleshooting	Tool & equipment control
Training & administration	Work site safety

Sample Cover Letter for a Repair Technician:

SAMUAL "Sam" JONES

729 Line Ave. – Middle Town, State 02021

Samjones44@email.com – (938) 555 – 3929

April 2, 2009

Greg Walters
Hiring Authority
Repairs USA
293 Main Street
Middle Town, State 02929

Dear Mr. Walters:

*Do you need someone who can walk into any household and inspire confidence and alleviate concerns? With the customer service I provide while serving as a **repair technician**, I have been doing exactly that for over ten years. I would like to provide your customers with that same level of service and am submitting my résumé for review in response to your advertisement in the Middle Town Gazette.*

With certifications in the installation and repair of heating, electrical, and power systems, I am fully qualified to meet the needs of your company. I have additional certifications for industrial building and am qualified to properly remove and dispose of outdated insulation if needed.

My fluency in Spanish has served me well in my career and I can communicate on a limited bases in Vietnamese, Korean, and Chinese.

I would appreciate the opportunity to meet with you to discuss in greater detail how my skills meet the needs of your company. I look forward to hearing from you to schedule an interview. Thank you for your time and consideration.

Regards,

Sam Jones

Sample Cover Letter for an Electrician:

JACK PAUL JONES

382 Fifth Place Blvd. — Las Vegas, NV 78392

Home: (282) 555-9839 — Cell: (282) 555-9292

May 1, 2009

Patrick Cunningham
Staff Coordinator
Any Corporation
564 Main St.
Las Vegas, NV 78659

Dear Mr. Cunningham:

I am currently investigating availabilities in electrical operations, and would like to submit my qualifications for your review.

*Although I am a newly licensed **journeyman electrician**, I have nine years of experience in the field — five as an apprentice and four as a journeyman. In my career, I've handled a variety of electrical installations while working with electrical contractors and as a subcontractor. I am capable of working independently or as a member of a team and feel confident in my ability to handle multiple responsibilities and provide quality performance on any project I undertake.*

The enclosed résumé is a brief summary of my experience. I would appreciate the opportunity to further discuss my qualifications, and with that in mind, I will contact your division next week to schedule a meeting. Thank you for your time and consideration.

Respectfully,

Jack Jones

Sample Cover Letter for Heavy Equipment Operator:

Jerry Radcliff
2871 Fifth Ave.
Mobile, AL 28392
(378) 555-2928

March 3, 2009

O'Malley Equipment and Moving
193 Richardson Road
Mobile, AL 28393

Dear Hiring Manager:

*With more than 17 years of experience as a **Heavy Equipment Operator**, I will be of great value to your company as you look to hire a site foreman. I am an experienced equipment trainer who has instructed dozens of students in proper use and safety on a variety of heavy machinery.*

I am proficient in the operation of:

- *Backhoe/ Front-End Loader*

- *Skid Loader*

- *Forklift (Standing, walk-behind, and articulating)*

- *Lift-All Telescopic Lift*

My administrative experience includes employee testing and evaluations, equipment maintenance, parts inspection, ordering and replacement, and safety protocols — creation and adherence. I have a strong work ethic that I impart on those who work with and for me. I am adaptable to changing environments, and I routinely finish work in the budgeted amount of time or earlier.

After you have reviewed my attached résumé, I hope to hear from you in order to schedule an interview. I appreciate your time and consideration.

Best regards,

Jerry

(This letter was written in Times New Roman at font size 12)

Teaching and Education Careers

Credentials: List them prominently — right after your contact information, if appropriate. You want to showcase what subject matters and grade levels you are qualified to teach immediately.

Experience: Mention the classes you have taught, including grade level and number of students. Include any information about special lesson plans, field trips, or guest speakers you have secured to help bring your subject matter to life for your students.

Committees: Mention any committees you have served on or any student organizations for which you have acted as faculty advisor.

Keywords and phrases:

Accreditation	Academic advising
Academic standards	Admissions management
Alumni relations	Campus life

Capital giving campaign	Career counseling & development
Classroom management	Course design
Curriculum development	Education services administration
Enrollment	Higher education
Holistic learning	Instructional materials and programming
Intercollegiate athletics	Leadership training
Management development	Multimedia learning methodologies
Parent-teacher relations	Peer counseling
Program development	Public/private partnerships
Public speaking	Research & publishing
Residential life	Scholastic standards
School administration	Seminar management
Student advisement	Student placement
Student recruitment	Student relations
Teacher training & instruction	Tenure
Testing and evaluation	Textbook review & selection

Cover Letter for a Teacher in response to an advertised position:

Sarah Mitchell

1492 Lee Road – Phoenix, AZ 83745 – (602) 555-9483

June 10, 2009

Patrick O'Hare
Principal
Smith High School

1493 Smith Blvd.
Tempe AZ 84732

Dear Mr. O'Hare:

I enjoyed our conversation regarding the history and government teaching position available at Smith High School. As you requested, I am forwarding my résumé, which details my credentials and experience.

I would like to draw your attention to a few highlights in my teaching career:

- My B.A. degree was earned at the University of Arizona, where I double majored in history and political science. My master's degree in education was obtained at UCLA.

- I am certified to teach in California and Arizona.

- I instructed American History, American Government, and World History at two high schools before my current position at East Side High School.

- At East Side, I instructed AP American History and AP American Government for the last three years. I am proud to say that my students routinely score threes and fours on the exams. This last year, five of my twenty students scored fives.

- I am the faculty advisor to the Young Republicans and Interact Club, and both organizations have raised funds for local charities and sent students to national conventions.

I enjoy my teaching position at East Side immensely, but recently, my mother's failing health has given me reason to move closer to *her, and your school is located less than five miles from her home. After you review my résumé, I would appreciate meeting with you to further discuss how my experience would benefit your program. I will contact you by the end of next week to schedule a time that is best for us to meet.*

Regards,

Sarah Mitchell

Sample Cover Letter for the High School Science Teacher:

JULIET SMITH

202 South Crabgrass Lane

Shady Hollow, GA 39202

(322) 555-03932

jsmith@email.com

August 17, 2009

Mr. Richard Townson
Principal
Shady Hollow High School
292 Robinson Road
Shady Hollow, GA 39202

Dear Principal Townson:

With five years of experience in teaching high school and a master's degree in biology, I believe I am an ideal candidate to fill the science teaching position you have open with the retirement of Bill Hayes.

My teaching experience was at Rose Garden High School in Rosewood before my husband and I moved here seven years ago. While there, I taught Advanced Placement Biology, Honors Biology, Advanced Placement Anatomy, Honors Anatomy, and Microbiology.

When we moved here I was pregnant with my oldest. Now that my youngest has started kindergarten, I am eager to return to the workforce. Although I focused on my family these last seven years and have not worked for pay, I kept up with developments in teaching and biology by reading literature and attending conferences hosted by the American Association of High School Science Instructors.

I look forward to raising my children in this community and someday teaching them at Shady Hollow High School. Please review my attached résumé. I will be contacting you next week to schedule an interview. Thank you for your consideration.

Best Regards,

Juliet Smith

Sample Cover Letter for an Elementary School Principal:

MATTHEW MORRISON

2827 Browning Drive – San Francisco CA 92829

(298) 555-9389 – mmorrison@email.com

December 31, 2009

Ms. Dottie Carrier
Hiring Committee
San Francisco Public Schools
899 Circle Drive
San Francisco, CA 92839

Dear Ms. Carrier:

I found your advertisement for an elementary school principal on website.com and wanted to take the opportunity to introduce myself through this letter.

With over 16 years of experience as an administrator and educator, I believe my qualifications are ideally matched to your requirements. My main teaching experience came in Ohio where I last worked as a principal at a Columbus middle school. When my wife and I moved here three years ago, I decided to go back into the classroom, and after passing my state certification test − I began teaching English and Creative Writing at Ridgemonte High School.

My attached résumé details the accomplishments of my career, but I would like to take this time to draw your attention to the following highlights:

- With booster club support, built a new computer lab at my former middle school that allowed our low-income student population training and access to today's technologies.

- Coordinated efforts with parents, teachers, and after-school tutors to raise the academic testing level of the students from failing to excellent in four years.

- Was honored as "Teacher of the Year" for the state of Ohio in 2000.

- Was honored as "Principal of the Year" for the state of Ohio in 2003.

I understand the open position is at a school in desperate need of improvements. Perhaps the most valuable skill I bring to the table is the ability to fund-raise and lobby government for money. I am confident my impact will be felt at that school after one academic year. I would like to discuss my candidacy further with you. Please contact me to schedule an interview at your earliest convenience.

Regards,

Matthew Morrison

(This letter was written in Times New Roman at font size 11)

Sample Cover Letter for a Guidance Counselor:

Elizabeth Doring

3982 Roberts Road — Austin TX 59302

(392) 555-9292 — edoring@email.com

Feb. 6, 2009

Principal Thomas Langley
Jefferson High School
3829 Education Lane
Austin TX 59839

Dear Mr. Langley:

In response to your advertisement for a guidance counselor, I would like to submit my résumé, which highlights 15 years of successful work with teens in a variety of mentoring positions. Additionally you will see a commitment to continued education so that I am on the forefront of my profession.

I began my career working with the Boys and Girls Clubs of America, and was on hand at the centers for children or teens that needed someone to confide in. The issues I counseled on ranged from sibling rivalry to drug abuse and teen pregnancy. It was a rewarding and challenging period where I attended many conferences and training to best serve my patients.

After my first child was born, I began work in the Western County School system as a high school guidance counselor. In the ten years since, it has been my honor to assist students in their academic pursuits and counsel them in their personal issues. One highlight from that time period was assisting a student who was reading and writing remedially in ninth grade because of an undiagnosed learning disability. After discovering her dyslexia and arranging for her to have tutors, and with deep commitment from her and her parents, she graduated with honors and is now attending Harvard Law School.

It was with sadness that I left Western High School, but after several months spent moving our household with my husband's job transfer, adjusting my children to their new schools, and establishing roots in the area through volunteer work, I am excited to apply for this position with you.

I look forward to meeting with you and will call you next week to schedule a time. Thank you for your consideration.

Regards,

Elizabeth Doring

Technology, Science, and Engineering Careers

Knowledge: Be sure to mention relevant technical knowledge for your specific industry, including experience with equipment, computer hardware and software, operating systems, and networks.

Research: Document any research papers, studies, or patents in which you have participated.

Projects: Discuss projects you have worked on, particularly ones you have headed up, and the results of those projects.

Keywords and phrases:

Applications development	Benchmark
Capital project	Computer-aided design & manufacturing
Cross-functional team	Customer management
Efficiency	Engineering design
Ergonomic techniques	Experimental design & methods
Fault analysis	Field performance
Information services management	Information technology
Methods design	Multimedia technology integration
OSHA – Occupational Safety & Health Administration.	Operating and maintenance
Performance optimization	Process design & development
Product innovation	Product reliability
Productivity improvement	Project management
Prototype development & testing	Quality assurance

Regulatory compliance	Research & development
Resource management	Root cause
Scale-up	Scientific methodologies
Specifications	Statistical analysis
Technical briefings	Technical writing
Types of engineering: aerospace, agricultural, biological, biomedical, chemical, computer, development, electrical, electronics, environmental, hardware, industrial, maintenance, manufacturing, materials, mechanical, nuclear, optics, software, systems & test	User training and support

Sample Cover Letter for a Chemical Buyer:

GEORGE McREYNOLDS
38 Park Street
City, State 22822
(342) 555-3929
gmcreynolds@email.com

May 1, 2009

Ms. Margaret Collins
Vice-President of Materials
National Industry
1 West 42nd Road
City, State 39201

Ms. Collins:

It appears that my qualifications are an excellent match for your advertised need for a chemicals buyer, which was posted in the

State Newspaper. Please accept the enclosed résumé for your review.

Allow me to highlight a few key points from my résumé that match your requirements:

- *B.S. degree in chemistry from State University.*

- *Five years of chemical purchasing experience.*

- *Excellent closure rate on long-term contracts at below-market rates.*

- *Talented negotiator with experience in million-dollar chemical contracts for four plan sites.*

My time spent as a buyer has taught me the importance of seeking out quality products. I once saved my company millions of dollars and a potential lawsuit by walking away from a questionable source that later proved to be providing substandard chemicals.

I am detail-oriented, do my research, and while concentrating on the bottom-line, I make my primary focus the procurement of quality product.

I look forward to meeting with you after you have had the opportunity to review the qualifications detailed in my résumé. Thank you for your time and consideration.

Sincerely,

George McReynolds

Sample Cover Letter for a Mechanical Engineer:

CHRISTINA WU

82 Harbor Road — City, State 39282

(392) 555-9939 — christinawu@email.com

April 3, 2009

Mr. Alexander Hayes

Hiring Manager

Contractors United

ahayes@email.com

Dear Mr. Hayes

In response to your advertisement for a mechanical engineer on website.com, I am submitting my résumé for your review. After you review my attached résumé, I believe you will find that my experience makes me a highly qualified candidate for this position.

After working my way through school, I completed my engineering degree at the University of North Carolina with a 3.7 GPA.

I then went to work for the state of North Carolina in their city development department. I spent five years there designing road systems and assisting the city planners in developing their blueprints. Five years ago, I relocated to Georgia, where I went to work for Big Corporation, designing their new plants.

During my ten years of employment at both locations, I consistently completed work under budget and ahead of schedule.

I will deliver the same performance for your company. I would like to schedule an interview with you at your earliest convenience, and I am looking forward to hearing from you in that regard.

Sincerely,

Christina Wu

(This letter was written in Verdana in font size 11)

Sample Cover Letter for a Research Analyst:

JAMAAL WASHINGTON
38 East Main Street Apt. 10
Baltimore, MD 29382

(410) 555-3920

March 3, 2009

Trish Robinson
Director
Lab Consulting
trobinson@email.com

Dear Ms. Robinson:

When I saw your advertisement on website.com for a senior research analyst, I knew my qualifications would be a great match to your listed requirements. With strengths in quantitative and qualitative research methods, and proven interpersonal and communication skills, I am confident my experience and expertise will be an immediate benefit to your organization.

Please allow me to highlight aspects from my attached résumé that speak directly to your advertisement:

- *Excellent analytical and report writing skills, with several publications in top scientific journals, including my Ph.D. thesis, which was published in Science Today (July 2001).*

- *Solid oral presentation skills highlighted by the presentation of my Ph.D. thesis at several scientific conferences, including the Southwest Research Association Conference in May of 2001.*

- *Over 15 years of experience in conducting, analyzing, and interpreting data in both my academic and professional career.*

- *Strong understanding of microbiology, contributing to scientific research and to the development of risk assessment methods for related research.*

- *Proven leadership and team management skills demonstrated in my current position as lab manager, where under my leadership, we have reduced injuries by five percent, increased efficiency by ten percent, and increased our accuracy rating to 99 percent.*

As a highly motivated, results-driven individual, I offer your organization decisive leadership, dedication, and a commitment to excellence. Thank you for your time and consideration of my application. I look forward to discussing in detail with you the ways in which I can bring significant value to your organization. Please feel free to contact me at your convenience.

Sincerely,

Jamaal Washington

Sample cover letter for an Electrical Engineer:

RICHARD LEMON
7 High Street
City, State 39282
(392) 555-9939
rlemon@email.com

June 6, 2009

Mr. Pete Carlton
Senior Site Manager
Builders USA
pcarlton@email.com

Dear Mr. Carlton,

In response to your advertisement for an Electrical Engineer on website.com, I am submitting my résumé for your review. My current employer has been hit hard by the economic downturn and is in the midst of a merger. As with any merger, who will stay with the company and who will be let go is uncertain. Therefore, I am exploring new career opportunities. I am looking for a position in Site Management to apply my skills and 22 years of engineering and management experience.

As a manager, I believe that since we spend so much of our lives in the workplace, work should be a pleasant experience and I strive to make it one for my team. I find that makes them more productive workers and increases efficiency. With 95 percent employee satisfaction rating and an average of 20 percent efficiency improvements yearly, my belief is supported with results. I would like to continue my success under your direction in Site Management.

If my management style is attractive to you, I would like to meet with you to further discuss my experience and why I would make a positive contribution to your team. Thank you for your consideration, and I look forward to hearing from you soon.

Best Regards,

Richard Lemon

(This letter was written in Verdana in font size 11)

Sample "cold call" cover letter:

JENNIFER LOHSL
382 Royal Court Circle
City, State 20291
(382) 555-2929
Jlohsl5380

July 5, 2009

Mr. Jack Webb
Director of Procurement
Plaxo Inc.
82 Line Street
City, State 29108

Dear Mr. Webb:

As you are probably aware, Wagner and Bushnell announced a cutback in the size of its area workforce by over 2,000 employees. Unfortunately, my position was one of the ones eliminated by the company.

Should you be in the market for a proven, energetic, and productive procurement manager for either a corporate or division-led assignment, I would welcome the opportunity to speak with you. A brief summary of my qualifications is as follows:

- *B.S. Chemical Engineering — Penn State*

- *Five years of procurement experience, advancing from associate buyer to managing buyer.*

- *Complete knowledge of all relevant computer software, including Microsoft Office.*

The details of my career are laid out more completely in my attached résumé. After you review it, I'm sure you will agree that I have a wide range of procurement experience over a varied range of products.

While I am focused on the bottom line, as shown by the savings I secured for Wagner and Bushnell, I am also focused on quality. With shrewd negotiating skills, I never sacrifice one for the other.

I look forward to talking with you soon regarding my ability to make a similar impact on your company. I will call you later in the week to schedule an interview at your convenience.

Sincerely,

Jennifer Lohsl

Cover Letter sample sent to a Headhunter for a Lab management professional:

John Smith
3333 Martin Hwy.
Thomas Town. FL 56575
Home (354) 555-6498 / Cell (354) 555-8389 / jsmith@email.com

January 1, 2009

Mr. Ben Anderson
Tech Placement Agency
1254 North Atlanta Blvd.
Jacksonville FL 34875

Dear Mr. Anderson,

If any of your clients would benefit from my 15 years of lab management experience, I would enjoy the opportunity to work with you. My attached résumé details my achievements in streamlining business processes, maintaining quality control, and governing production and testing in a lab environment.

The core of my experience stems from an analytical perspective – concentration testing, flow-to-background testing, durability testing, and sensitivity testing while managing teams that were both creative and talented to produce highly focused, yet technology-driven labs.

As a manager, I was exceptionally rated with a talent for improving work through monitoring quality performance. I also understand that to build up a solid team, you must do it through sound operational processes and well-maintained logistics and procurement.

Evidence of my contributions can be seen through my success in:

- Managing the daily operations of a lab that manufactures non-destructive testing materials as dictated by military specifications. Our government contracts were fulfilled ahead of schedule and below budget, which is why we were awarded a new one every fiscal year.

- Overseeing several departments, including research and development where I participated in over ten research projects that later led to successful company patents.

- Continual monitoring of employee performance with a deep commitment to process and productivity – which improved consistently every year under my leadership at each lab I ran.

With my scientific degrees, I am looking to transition into senior-level laboratory management. If you have any clientele that have such an opening, I hope you will recommend me for that position. Please be advised that my target salary range is $60,000-$70,000. I am willing to travel, but cannot consider relocation at this time.

I realize it is important to get a feel for a person and believe a face-to-face meeting would be the best way for you to do that with me. I will contact you shortly to schedule a time that is convenient for us to meet.

Regards,

John Smith

Cover Letter from a graduating Engineering Student to a Head-hunting Agency:

EMMA BROWN

(847) 555-2827 — ebrown45@email.com

Current Address:	*Permanent Address:*
198 South Hall — FSU	*2837 Lakeside Drive*
Tallahassee FL 38973	*Tampa FL 32729*

March 15, 2009

Howard Wright
Job Placement Associates
7892 Lime Street Suite 9B
Tampa FL 34821

Dear Mr. Wright:

I am an honors engineering student at Florida State University and will be graduating with a bachelor's of science in mechanical engineering in May of this year.

I am in search of an entry-level position as a project engineer in the central engineering department of a manufacturing company. I would enjoy being involved with engineering, installation, and start-up of manufacturing equipment, as well as general plant facilities engineering work.

Besides my academic achievement, I am a student athlete who has played on the school's tennis team for the last three years. I have a balanced perspective and maintain involvement in a wide range of diverse activities.

Last summer, I was an engineering intern with The Armor Hammer Company, where I worked in their central engineering department as an apprentice to the design engineer in support of plant capital projects. My supervisor will gladly serve as a referral, as will several of my professors.

Should one of your client companies have room in their organization for a bright, eager engineer, I would appreciate a call. Thank you for your time and consideration.

Sincerely

Emma Brown

(This letter was written in Bookman Old Style in font size 10.5)

CHAPTER 11

Samples by Experience

C hapter ten provided the reader with sample cover letters from various industries, but those samples could not account for all the variations of a person's career. Cover letters will vary widely depending on experience and skill level. This chapter will provide the reader with sample cover letters for the wide-range of experience that individuals may possess.

Two things are important to note when examining experience:

1. How to make yourself appear competitive. As this book goes to publication, the reported nationwide unemployment rate is 8 percent. In some areas, it is double-digits. The outcome of that economic reality are that people are taking jobs for which they are overqualified. If you are new to the job market, this can be an intimidating situation where you try to position yourself against people with greater experience than you. However, a well-written cover letter can allow you to show your employer that you will be a better long-term investment than your competition. Conversely, those with many years of experience may be con-

cerned about being overlooked for competition that is less qualified but may be a better financial value. Your goal is to demonstrate the immediate positive impact you will have on the company and that they will indeed get what they pay for.

2. Find the right balance between "fluff" and "figures." There is an inverse relationship between experience and fluff. The more you have of the first, the less you are expected to present of the second. A person with a great deal of experience should never fluff a cover letter or résumé. Hiring authorities will expect to see hard figures to back up your years of experience, and nothing less. Remembering this important distinction can make the difference between impressing a hiring authority and having them pass you by.

As you decide where you fall on the experience scale, remember that there is one main message to convey in your cover letter: "This is what I can do for you!"

A company is never going to hire you in order for you to have a place to retire or to advance your career with training opportunities. Therefore, your cover letter should convey what you can do for them, how quickly you can do it, and, without mentioning salary (unless absolutely necessary), leave them with an impression of what type of compensation you expect to be paid.

Tell Employers What You Can Do for Them.

Quantify this as much as possible. If you are just starting out, talk about the results you expect to achieve for the company. If you have mid-to-high-level experience, use past performance as an indicator of future productivity. Point to your prior success to demonstrate to the hiring authority exactly what you can do for them.

Tell Employers How Quickly You Can Make a Difference.

If you are just starting out in your career and industry, training or corporate training will be necessary — don't ignore that fact. Just don't treat this training like it's an opportunity for you, even though it is. Your potential employer knows this, but you don't want to leave them with the impression that they are going to train you just so you can leave them for a better position somewhere else. Instead, tell them how their training is going to pay off. Talk about how quickly you will produce results after your training is complete.

Mid-to-high-level job seekers should emphasize that they can produce immediate results. This is especially true for executives. The company that hires you will expect results starting the day you are hired. Tell them in your cover letter that this is exactly what you plan to provide.

Tell Employers Your Expectations.

Let me make this clear: I am *not* saying tell them a salary, or even the salary range you expect to be paid. You may at times have to do that, but not if it is avoidable.

What I am suggesting is that you use buzz words like "entry-level," "mid-level management," or "senior executive" to indicate the type of position and compensation for which you are applying. This is less necessary in responses to an advertised position.

But when producing "cold call" letters, it is an important thing to consider.

Consider how the following examples contrast from entry to executive-level cover letters.

Sample Cover Letter for an Entry-Level Position:

PAMALA BROWN

1837 8th Ave. Belleview FL 34828

(847) 555-2827 ---- pbrown45@email.com

May 15, 2009

Howard Wright
Parts-n-Things
hwright@email.com

Dear Mr. Wright:

*I saw your advertisement for an entry-level **project engineer** in Engineering Monthly, and I wanted to take this opportunity to send you my résumé and tell you a bit about myself.*

I recently graduated sigma cum laude from Florida State University with a B.S. in mechanical engineering, where I made As in all of my core engineering courses.

I spent last summer in Michigan interning with the Armor Hammer Company in their central engineering department as an apprentice to the design engineer in support of plant capital projects. My supervisor will gladly serve as a referral, as will several of my professors.

With a solid education and excellent hands-on training, I expect to be one of your top project engineers this year. I will gladly relocate, and my salary requirements range from $35,000-$40,000.

Thank you for taking the time to consider my résumé. I look forward to hearing from you soon.

Sincerely,

Pamala Brown

Enclosure: Résumé and transcripts.

Sample Cover Letter for an Experienced Human Resources Director:

Alexander Matthews, SPHR
783 West Main Street Apt 134 – West Town, NC 82724
(463) 555 – 9282

Feb. 23, 2008

Daniel Chamberlain
Toys Warehouse
dchamberlain@email.com

Dear Mr. Chamberlain:

*You recent advertisement on website.com for **head of human resources** captured my interest because your needs and my background are a close match.*

As a human resource director with more than 15 years of experience, I have worked for companies that ranged in size from 100 to

3,000. I am known for creating customer service-oriented organizations that remained focused on bottom-line results. My career accomplishments include successfully re-engineering departments to make them more streamlined and in touch with today's technologies, as well as corporate recruiting, staffing, and employee development programs.

Please note that while directing the overall human resource department, I also remain up-to-date in all core HR functions, including new state regulations and procedures to ensure that all paperwork is being filled out and properly filed.

My major projects have included benefits/compensation design, HRIS selection and implementation, and large-scale recruitment activities in business pre-opening situations (over 2,500 employees recruited).

I would welcome the opportunity to speak with you more in depth about your needs and how I can contribute immediately to your success. I will follow up in the next few days to ensure that you received my materials and answer any preliminary questions you may have.

Best regards,

Alexander Matthews

Enclosure: Résumé

Sample Cover Letter for an Executive Level Sales Position:

Amber Smith
837 Mill Street – Colorado City, Colorado 98372
(827) 555- 2928 - asmith@email.com

Feb. 24, 2009

Mr. Rob Patterson
Sales R Us
rpatterson@email.com

Dear Mr. Patterson:

*Sales and marketing is about developing and implementing an innovative and tactical vision that will generate outstanding results and profitability. My leadership abilities and extensive hands-on experience will benefit you as your **sales director** because I will produce a vision that inspires your staff to not only meet, but to exceed your expectations. I have attached my résumé for your consideration.*

Promoted to increasingly challenging and responsible positions, I mastered the following skills in my 26 years of experience:

- *Leadership: With an excellent record in recruitment, motivation, and performance of sales team, I currently manage a team of nine that has exceeded their margin target by 10 to 30 percent each fiscal quarter for three years.*

- *Business development: I demonstrated the ability to asses a marketplace and uncover new clients in my current and last position, increasing clientele for both businesses by 25 percent over five years.*

- *Relationship management: I possess solid skills in forging and solidifying client, partner, and vendor relationships. This is demonstrated by my proven negotiating skills in writing over 30 new contracts per year for the last five years.*

My skills at leading sales teams to conceptualize, build, and implement ground-breaking marketing strategies will bring Sales R Us from the number four slot to the number one slot in the industry in six months. I am excited by the opportunity to meet with you and will contact you shortly to schedule an interview at your earliest convenience.

Best regards,

Amber Smith

Another Cover Letter for an experienced sales professional:

Margaret "Peg" Mitchell

393 West 5th Street – Bloomburg, CT 23728 – (284) 555-2929

April 13, 2009

Dear Mr. Jonathan Franklin:

With documented success forging strategic relationships to maximize revenue growth, I am writing in response to your search for a senior sales representative. Skilled in product knowledge, troubleshooting, competitive advantage, construction project management, customer needs, and logistics/procurement/ delivery, I will be a valuable asset within your organization.

During my 15 plus years of experience, I turned around an underperforming distribution center, enabling the branch to rank within the 15 top branches among 65 locations. In addition, I decreased inventory from $2.9 million to $500,000, increased revenue 300 percent in two years, and drove sales from $200,000 to $2 million in five years. I am confident I will equally impact your company.

Moreover, I maintain in-depth product knowledge to boost overall customer satisfaction and deliver new, repeat, and referral business. Eager to detail my achievements and discuss your strategic plans, I look forward to your reply. Meanwhile, thank you for your attention.

Sincerely,

Peg Mitchell

Enclosure

(Prepared by contributor Danny Huffman)

Compare and Contrast Experience

The entry level cover letter:

The first cover letter was written by a college graduate seeking an entry-level position. The writer makes note of that in the cover letter and includes a typical salary range for a starting position in that industry. Not typically recommended, but in this particular case it works to notify the hiring authority what type of position the job seeker is applying to. This is done to assure the hiring authority that while they might have to provide the individual with training, they are receiving a value for their efforts.

The cover letter makes note of an outstanding academic career, along with an internship that provides hands-on experience. This is done so that the hiring manager knows the quality of the applicant's learning ability. If a company anticipates you will need some training, it is best to assure them that you are an exceptional student. This gives them the idea that even if they do not see immediate results from you, they will see results soon that exceed their expectations.

The mid-level cover letter:

The second cover letter is for a person mid-career seeking to advance. The mid-level career cover letter shows how the writer has several years of experience in the field and is qualified to advance to the next level of management and responsibility. The writer makes several references to job performance that the hiring director can identify as something he/she would like to see out of a candidate. The writer also confidently states that he will make an immediate impact in the job, which is something any hiring authority wants to see.

The executive level cover letter:

In the third cover letter sample, the writer demonstrates more specifically the job skills that will contribute to the success of the company. Additionally, the writer talks about not only the positive impact hiring them will make on the company but a specific reference to how she will change the company's standing in the industry.

The fourth letter is also for the executive level and demonstrates how to quantify what skills and experience you bring to the table as an applicant. The hiring authority examining the fourth cover letter has a definite sense of what the writer can do for his or her company if employed.

CHAPTER 12

Samples for the Challenging Résumé

The final chapter of this book will offer sample cover letters and advice for people who will have the most difficult time convincing hiring directors to look over their résumés. These recommendations will address the following situations:

- Career changes

- "On-ramping"

- Returning to work after illness

- Job hunting after being laid off

Career Change

When you are seeking to change careers for whatever reason, you should be looking forward rather than back. Your résumé and cover letter should focus on your future career objectives and how the skills you have acquired thus far have prepared you for such an opportunity.

It has been discussed in previous chapters how important key terminology is in writing cover letters. It is possible that you looked over those lists of keywords and phrases and did not find many of them that applied to you. Take a second look. Sometimes the most difficult thing to do in a career change is recognize the skills you already possess and how they can translate to a new line of work.

Finding new ways to say old things:

The military is infamous for its acronyms and how officers and soldiers learn to speak in what they call "alphabet soup." But the military isn't the only business that comes with its own set of slang and verbal shortcuts. It is important to eliminate these phrases from your cover letter when making a career change. Assume that your target audience — the hiring authority — does not understand your business shorthand and spell out what you want to say.

The Military:

One of the most difficult career changes is the transition from the military to the civilian workforce. The most important thing to remember when writing a résumé or cover letter under this circumstance is to phrase your skills and accomplishments in civilian terminology.

Non-Profit to Private Industry:

The two entities have more in common than you might recognize at first. Implementing a budget is the same in any industry. Constituency service is customer service, and fund-raising is sales.

The most important thing you can do is recognize that even though the skills needed to operate in these two separate worlds are the same, the buzz words are different. Know your audience and use the appropriate language for the position for which you are applying.

Academia:

Another common career change is the transition into or out of teaching. No matter what level, the skills needed for an education career do transition well to other careers. For example, student instruction and corporate training have many similarities.

Additionally, while teaching accreditation may be required, real-world experience often appeals to educational institutions for the insight it offers students.

"On-Ramping"

In 2004, the Hidden Brain Drain Task Force was launched to address the issue of women and minorities in the workforce as unrealized assets. As a member of the task force, Sylvia Hewett took their findings and published the book *Off-Ramps and On-Ramps: Keeping Talented Women on the Road to Success in 2007.*

The findings of the task force indicate that many professional women will take a break in their careers — one that is usually related to having children — which is considered their "off-ramp." "On-ramping" is the process women (and sometimes men) go through to get back on their career track.

The task of "on-ramping" can be a difficult one. Even in an era where employers advertise that they are "family friendly," Huffman still says that employers may be concerned that a candidate will have to call in due to a sick child and other such problems.

"Unfortunately, stating one was away from work due to rearing of children is seen as a negative and many will disqualify this candidate immediately," he explained. Huffman's advice is to not mention kids or explain why you were taking time off in your cover letter. You can address those questions in an interview.

However, Vivian Steir Rabin, coauthor of *Back on the Career Track*, had different advice to offer women in her online article, "What to do about cover letters and references if you haven't worked in years," posted July 4, 2008.

Rabin advised that if you have a gap in your résumé, explain it in your cover letter. She said to do it briefly and unashamedly with a line like:

> *Although I focused on my family these last five years and have not worked for pay, I kept up with development in my field by reading Business Woman Magazine and attending conferences hosted by Business Daily.*

She says the key to successful "on-ramping" is making it clear to employers that you are ready to start back on the career track with enthusiasm and that you have the skills to do so.

Rabin advises not to bring up salary at all in a cover letter or interview and advises instead to wait until the employer addresses the subject. She says to not worry about references in your cover letter or résumé, but if you have been out of work for several years, she suggests making contact early with old bosses and colleagues to bring yourself to the forefront of their mind. This way they can speak well on your behalf when a prospective employer does call.

Unanimous advice for moms looking to "on-ramp," is to focus on volunteer work during the employment gap. Much like when a student wants to use campus activities in a cover letter and résumé, volunteer work should be used to demonstrate leadership, organizational skills, or fund-raising abilities. Approach your volunteer work from a business viewpoint.

Ask yourself the following questions:

- Did you help an organization make or save money?

- Did you help an organization run more efficiently?

- Did you manage or organize events or fund-raisers?

- Did you create literature or processes that will be used by future members of the organization?

All of these activities can be used to show skills that are highly valued in the corporate world. Also, remember to show your target audience your skills rather than simply state a title. For example, do not simple state that you were president of the PTA.

Instead say:

> Under my leadership as president of the Parent/Teacher Association, we grew our membership by 15 percent and raised over $150,000, which among other projects funded a new computer lab at the school. We also started a volunteer after-school tutoring program that raised school testing scores by 20 percent overall.

A tip for résumé writing for "on-ramping" moms or dads is to place volunteer work at the top of your résumé to highlight your most recent accomplishments.

Finally, "on-ramping" moms should remember to draw on past work experience, even if it seems dated. That was valuable work experience and should not be discarded, even if it is years old.

Returning to Work After Illness or Disability

For people who have been out of work due to extended illness or physical disability, it is important to focus on what you can do for the employer, not what you can't. It would not be ideal for any person to focus on a negative detail in their cover letter, and you should not do it either. Be positive and deal with any special work requirements once you land your interview.

A friend of mine, Shay-Anne Matthews, went through a traumatic downturn in health when the diabetes she had been dealing with her whole life got significantly worse in her early 20s. After two transplant surgeries and the loss of her eyesight, she knows the difficultly of addressing these concerns when looking for employment.

But she says not to mention disabilities in a cover letter. "You know your limitations, so only apply for positions you know you can handle. That way, when you go in for an interview you are fully prepared to explain how you will be successful despite your disability," she said.

The important thing to remember when returning to work after a long absence is, while you may have to start in a lower position than your age contemporaries that pursued careers, the skills you acquired outside of the workforce will aide you in your advancement. That is the message your want to convey in your cover letter.

Been Laid Off

The economic times we live in mean that people have been laid off. The stigma of this is quickly disappearing. "With eight percent plus unemployment, this is not an uncommon situation, and employers are more and more sensitive to the fact," said Huffman.

"But *never* state negatives in a cover letter or during an interview," he added. "If, during an interview, the hiring agent asks specific questions about reasons for job hunting, always be honest, always portray in the positive, and never become angry, stressed, or disrespectful to previous employers."

Another tip for dealing with periods of unemployment in the past is to simply put the years you were employed with a company on your résumé. Huffman said that specific dates are no longer required.

If you choose to mention your layoff in your cover letter despite Huffman's suggestion, the cover letter on the following page demonstrates one way to approach that subject.

Sample Cover Letters

The cover letters on the following pages address one or more of the above situations and the recommendations previously discussed.

Sample cover letter addressing the lay-off question:

JENNIFER LOHSL
382 Royal Court Circle
City, State 20291
(382) 555-2929
Jlohsl5380

July 5, 2009

Mr. Jack Webb
Director of Procurement
Plaxo Inc.
82 Line Street
City, State 29108

Dear Mr. Webb:

As you are probably aware, Wagner and Bushnell announced a cutback in the size of its area workforce by over 2,000 employees. Unfortunately, my position was one of the ones eliminated by the company.

Should you be in the market for a proven, energetic, and productive procurement manager for either a corporate or division-led assignment, I would welcome the opportunity to speak with you. A brief summary of my qualifications are as follows:

- *B.S. Chemical Engineering – Penn State*

- *Five years of procurement experience, advancing from associate buyer to managing buyer.*

- *Complete knowledge of all relevant computer software including Microsoft Office.*

The details of my career are laid out more completely in my attached résumé. After you review it, I'm sure you will agree that I have a wide range of procurement experience over a varied range of products.

While I am focused on the bottom line, as shown by the savings I secured for Wagner and Bushnell, I am also focused on quality. With shrewd negotiating skills, I never sacrifice one for the other.

I look forward to talking with you soon regarding my ability to make a similar impact on your company. I will call you later in the week to schedule an interview at your convenience.

Sincerely,

Jennifer Lohsl

Sample cover letter for a person changing careers:

MARK WEBB
33 Line Blvd.   *(332) 555-3990*
City, State 29302   *mwebb@email.com*

September 22, 2009

Bill Harper
Hiring Manager
Research USA
81559 Rosewood Court
City, State 29382

Dear Mr. Harper:

Although I am employed in management, my long-term interest has always been market research. In my employment at Survey

Data, Inc., I combined my backgrounds in sales and my education in research development to lead a highly productive sales team who provided exceptional customer service to clients.

Our team, more so than any other, could provide in-depth answers to clients' questions regarding why they needed our data and how they could use it long term. After eight years in the industry, I have a track record highlighted with consistent bottom-line contributions, exceeding sales quotas, and pro-active problem solving initiatives.

Your company has well-known marketing strategies and I would welcome the opportunity to join your team. While it would be my goal to transition to your research department team, I believe my sales and customer service experience would be useful when presenting information to your sales team and clients.

In addition to providing customer service personally, I can train your sales team to provide the same exceptional service mine did at Survey Data, Inc. With experience in writing training material and classroom instruction, you will find me a valuable asset in that regards.

In addition to these qualities, I am fluent in Spanish and able to travel with ease. I believe these skills will transition well to work as a research manager for your company. I would like to meet with you to discuss the benefits I can bring to Research USA. I can make myself available at your convenience and will call you next week to schedule an appointment. Thank you for your consideration.

Sincerely,

Mark Webb

Sample cover letter for the "on-ramping" mom:

JULIET SMITH
202 South Crabgrass Lane
Shady Hollow, GA 39202
(322) 555-03932
jsmith@email.com

August 17, 2009

Mr. Richard Townson
Principal
Shady Hollow High School
292 Robinson Road
Shady Hollow, GA 39202

Dear Principal Townson:

With five years of experience in teaching high school and a master's degree in biology, I believe I am an ideal candidate to fill the science teaching position you have open with the retirement of Bill Hayes.

My teaching experience was at Rose Garden High School in Rosewood before my husband and I moved here seven years ago. While there, I taught Advanced Placement Biology, Honors Biology, Advanced Placement Anatomy, Honors Anatomy, and Microbiology.

When we moved here, I was pregnant with my oldest. Now that my youngest has started kindergarten, I am eager to return to the workforce. Although I focused on my family these last seven years and have not worked for pay, I kept up with developments in teaching and biology by reading literature and attending conferences hosted by the American Association of High School Science Instructors.

I look forward to raising my children in this community and someday teaching them at Shady Hollow High School. Please review my attached résumé. I will be contacting you next week to schedule an interview. Thank you for your consideration.

Best Regards,

Juliet Smith

CONCLUSION

It doesn't matter if you are just starting out on a career path, "on-ramping," or have years of experience to showcase; the advice in this book should help you assemble a stunning cover letter that will grab the attention of your target audience and aide you in your quest for a new job.

Many of the cover letters in these pages were prepared by people I know in their individual industries. The rest were assembled by me per the advice of professionals like Danny Huffman and my own experiences.

My early work as a student editor and the education I received while gaining my B.S. in journalism made me a quality writer. But it was my experience as a teaching assistant while earning my master's degree in political science at the University of Florida that trained my eye to recognize bad writing. Later, my work as an adjunct professor at Cameron University in Lawton, Oklahoma, honed that skill to a greater degree. It is through those experiences that I assembled most of my writing recommendations in this book — particularly the errors to avoid.

I discovered through my teaching experience that the art of writing has been neglected in many people's educations. However, one does not need to be a professional writer to communicate effectively through the written word. A well-written, one-page cover letter that makes an impact is certainly within your grasp. The pages of this book hopefully aided you in that achievement.

I believe you will find that as you write, you will become a better writer. Therefore, if it takes you some time to assemble your first cover letter, do not be dismayed. As you continue your job search, letters will become easier with practice. You may never come to love writing cover letters, but hopefully you will find them easier to write now. Additionally, you may find other letters, such as referrals for people who contact you for networking, infinitely easier to prepare.

It writing this book, I hope I did more than just offer you advice for writing cover letters. Hopefully, I helped you expand your job search methods and prevented possible stumbling blocks on your road to success.

Remember that while your cover letter is your first step in the job acquisition process, there will be many others. Much of the advice in this book will aide you in the steps that follow. The research you did to prepare your letter will help you in your interview. The same attention to detail you spent on your letter should be given to your interview and subsequent negotiations. I wish you much success, not only making yourself the "best fit" for your potential employer, but also finding the job that is the "best fit" for you.

AUTHOR BIOGRAPHY

Kimberly Sarmiento has her M.A. in political campaigning and a B.S. in journalism from the University of Florida. She worked as an adjunct professor and freelance writer covering a range of subjects from sports to features to city government. She loves all writing and feels inspired to make the chore of writing a joy for others. She has two beautiful, energetic children who inspire her daily.

CONTRIBUTORS

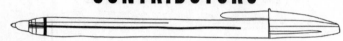

Jennifer Cassella
Office Administrator
Tyre and Taylor Commercial
Reality

Sonya Dutcher
Technical Account Manager
Quest Software

Amy Van Fossen
Lawyer
Poe & Freireich, P.A.

Danny Huffman
Professional Résumé Writer
Career Services Inc.

Shira Karp
Awards Analyst, Contractor
Military Awards Branch

Shay-Anne Matthews
Master's Student
Political Science and Sociology
University of Central Florida

Shannon Bow O'Brien, PhD
Professor
University of Texas

Allison Shvets
Sales Representative

INDEX